How to Write
a Chiller Thriller

How to Write
a Chiller Thriller

Sally Spedding

**COMPASS
BOOKS**

Winchester, UK
Washington, USA

First published by Compass Books, 2014
Compass Books is an imprint of John Hunt Publishing Ltd., Laurel House, Station Approach,
Alresford, Hants, SO24 9JH, UK
office1@jhpbooks.net
www.johnhuntpublishing.com
www.compass-books.net

For distributor details and how to order please visit the 'Ordering' section on our website.

Text copyright: Sally Spedding 2013

ISBN: 978 1 78279 172 0

A CIP catalogue record for this book is available from the British Library.

Design: Stuart Davies

Printed and bound by CPI Group (UK) Ltd, Croydon, CR0 4YY

We operate a distinctive and ethical publishing philosophy in all
areas of our business, from our global network of authors to
production and worldwide distribution.

CONTENTS

For Suzanne Ruthven and Merric Davidson for their support and encouragement.

Introduction

Chiller is short for spine-chiller, which means a book, film, etc, that arouses terror.

A thriller means a book, film, play, etc, which depicts a crime, mystery or espionage in an atmosphere of excitement and suspense.

So why do the many published and often hyped-up chiller thrillers fail to deliver the goods? Or am I and other readers just too picky?

Some say there are too many books being printed. And now we have Kindle, Nook, Smashwords, and others to fill the ether as well. In my view, it's not a question of too many books, but generally, in the crime and thriller genres, their sameness. Yet these categories remain hugely popular and most literary agents and publishers include them in their submission requirements. This is why, in writing this book with its many examples and exercises, my emphasis will be on encouraging you to dare to be different; to stand out from this often predictable material, where the successful author has become a 'brand,' and sadly, it's often hard to tell one of their thrillers from the other.

This is not only a deeply cynical but stifling trend, and personally, I would rather knit a scarf than be told – as a friend of mine once was - to ape a best-selling author of blood-soaked action involving South London gangsters. Someone she'd never even bothered to read. I discovered during my many talks to readers' groups, that they also felt sold short by mainstream publishers, and preferred to seek out their own gems. It's word of mouth by groups such as these that can be more lasting than relentless publisher promotion before their latest books' launch dates. I'm sure you know of interesting examples of titles where this has happened. *The Girl with the Dragon Tattoo*, for instance, with its flawed, truly original heroine, Lisbeth Salander. An embattled journalist who risks his career to defend her. The bleak settings in a relatively unfamiliar country. An evil father and other ruthless enemies make this a truly chilling thriller.

Sharp Objects by Gillian Flynn also sneaked on the scene, by way of a CWA John Creasey (New Blood) Dagger Award, bringing another memorable protagonist in the form of reporter Camille Preaker who returns to her former home in Missouri to investigate the murders of two local girls. From her weird mother, to the adjacent pig farm, this chiller has it all.

So, I'm about to fling open a few more metaphorical doors, by encouraging you to begin the journey by dredging yourselves. Your experiences, observations and imaginations, interests, deepest fears and greatest joys - all unique to you - will be crucial in creating original chiller thrillers to haunt your adult, even YA readers' minds long afterwards.

Also crucial, is an abiding curiosity in those who share our planet. About what we read and hear about them in the media or on our travels. A high-profile crime story or conspiracy theory will bring out the armchair detectives and pundits like moles after rain! Be nosy. Weigh up the (often inadequate/one-sided) information given and do some digging of your own to get the whole story. Everyone, from the seemingly ordinary man next door, to a Head of State has secrets. Some are minor, but some, if known, could have seismic consequences. I often ask those aspiring writers attending my workshops, "who needs fiction?" However, I also believe that this so-called 'fiction' carries truth in its belly.

There are and have been many investigative authors, broadcasters and journalists from all over the world who have risked their lives by exposing what they believe their fellow human beings ought to know. Some have been found dead in unexplained circumstances. Others warned off. I'm proud to be linked to the thriller genre with my own work because great expectations ride on its shoulders. Hidden worlds in the broadest sense, can be exposed. Future possibilities explored. Taboos too, which vary from one culture to another. Amongst all this, I'd like to think that thriller writers through their fiction, convey truth, and themselves retain a strong moral compass.

Only recently, did the Irish Prime Minister apologize for the suffering endured by thousands of young girls and women locked up in his country's workhouses as a punishment for petty crime or even homelessness. Survivors have formed the JFM (Justice For Magdalenes) and found at least 988 graves in laundry plots in cemeteries throughout Ireland. Those who never came out.

These are tough women. Just as Julie Bailey, crusading on behalf of her late mother and all those patients who needlessly died in their hospital beds.

My own *noir* thriller, *Malediction*, set in France during 1997, the European Year Against Racism, takes the theme of a mother desperate to find her missing student son. Yet she's up against a powerful, corruptible Church whose five priests, all damaged except one, form a cell to plot terrorist attacks against wealthy Jews 'staining' French soil. Their secret organization reaches the highest echelons of NATO while its black tentacles spread ever wider.

So, although this most exciting of genres continues to embrace crime, horror, historical, the paranormal, financial, political, futuristic, literary, erotic, romantic and even the comedies of Mike Ripley, it can be distinguished simplistically as dealing with the conflict between good and evil. E.g., in political thrillers, wherever set, in whatever time, a lone whistleblower - usually male - will attempt to unearth secrets that carry huge implications for all. Kathryn Bigelow's recent film *Zero Dark Thirty* based on the actual tracking and killing of Osama bin Laden, and featuring a dogged female journalist, makes for inspiring fictional material. Keep your eyes and ears open for docudramas that blend the two. Their construction can often be invaluable.

In conspiracy thrillers, yet more dogged heroes - again, mostly male - come up against a powerful, often secret enemy; some shadowy, sinister organization in which 'guilty-looking innocents' and 'innocent-looking guilties' may not be as they seem.

In spy thrillers, the stakes are again high, with settings varying from a mediaeval Tuscan Monastery in Umberto Eco's *The Name of the Rose* to Victorian lamplit streets and present-day Iran. From the Pentagon to an Al Quaeda base in Mali. While famous, real-life spies such as Kim Philby and Anthony Blunt came through the public school system and university, your own spy could be the unlikeliest one yet! Real life events can also trigger inspiration in this sub-genre. E.g., a young Australian immigrant, recruited by Mossad and charged with serious crimes, was recently found hanged in an Israeli jail. Why? No-one yet knows. But it's an intriguing case. As is the death of wealthy Russian Alexander Perepilichnyy found dead in November 2012 while out jogging in leafy Weybridge in Surrey And all the while, the master, John le Carré is still digging this rich seam where betrayal is the name of the game, and where it takes a certain dark psychology linked to money, threats and blackmail, for someone to 'shop' their nearest and dearest. Even their whole community. Apparently, angry wives make the most forthcoming informants, and instead of schlepping around Timbuktu or Dagestan, most MI6 intelligence staff are at their London desks mired in the humdrum chores of emails and memos.

"But it's all been done," you might complain. Not true. The key is passion. *Your* passion.

It's hard to keep pace with all the rapid developments in technology, but if this thrills you, then explore its exciting possibilities. Hot off the press is software which can, courtesy of Facebook and Twitter, track a person's movements and predict future behavior. There is also Germ Tracker, an app developed by scientists at Rochester University, USA, which tells users which places to avoid. All potential for an original chiller thriller, while MI5 has recently warned that terrorists can now slip through the net because intelligence agencies can't monitor their latest communications systems. And we all know where computer hacking can lead. Julian Assange may not be able to freely walk the streets for a long time yet. To some he's a hero, to others, a serious danger. He's not the first to fall foul of powerful governments, and won't be the last.

Minority Report based on Philip K. Dick's short story, where crime is predicted by psychics before it happens, is another chilling idea. As is recent research claiming that certain faces with particular dimensions, reveal their owners to be racist, while Cambridge University, has successfully scanned an image of a face into a 3D Face of the Future. The result is extraordinary, while Michael Marshall Smith's futuristic thrillers continue to disturb and shock. *Reviver*, by Seth Patrick sees the recently dead revived to testify as to how they were killed, and by whom.

Powerful also best describes the paranormal. A sub-genre that continues to chill many readers of both non-fiction and fiction. In Susan Hill's chiller, *The Woman in Black* and my own *Wringland*, *Cloven* and *Cold Remains*, mere mortals must outwit a force greater and more enduring than themselves. Rarely benign. Often deadly. You only have to read the Classical scholar, M.R. James to be spooked for life. Although he claimed never to have experienced the paranormal at first hand, the variety and believability of his ghostly manifestations is remarkable. As are his settings and erudition. Should you choose to write a paranormal thriller, your brief is to be as brave and inventive as he.

Unlike him, many of us have experienced profoundly life-changing occurrences involving disturbing séances, near-death experiences, angels good and bad and even stranger manifestations, yet enthusiastically we seek out such books. Why? Perhaps because we, in this so-called 'civilized' and mostly ordered world, have glimpsed something beyond our control. Shadows that haunt us from the moment of birth. Even perhaps before birth.

In May 2006, paranormal researchers were due to investigate Devonport Naval Base, focusing on the haunted Hangman's Cell where more than a hundred men were said to have been executed. These investigations are happening all the time, and the poor nun walled up in Borley Church can still be heard sighing.

In a Malvern second-hand bookshop, *The Scole Experiment* by Grant & Jane Solomon, in association with the Scole Experimental Group, practically fell off the shelf into my hands. Its subtitle reads, 'Scientific Evidence for Life After Death' and it details the results of a five-year investigation from the beginning of 1993 in which a group of psychic researchers and healers conducted a series of experiments in a farmhouse cellar in the Norfolk town of Scole. So incredible were the findings that senior members of the Society for Psychical Research, astrophysicists and electrical engineers asked if they could also observe, test and record what took place. Discarnate beings including Thomas Edison and possibly the German poet Friedrich Rückert, made direct contact by handwritten messages appearing on factory-sealed, unopened photographic film. Objects were apported and solid beings regularly appeared. Ultimately, the research ended because certain entities became too dominant and destructive.

This is a truly life-changing book and a great resource for any author writing in the paranormal sub-genre. The discarnate don't merely have to be seen. They can be heard or smelt, with powers not only to influence technology. The late Arthur Guirdham, a well-known child psychologist and author, is also worth attention for his regression of a seven year-old schoolgirl from Bath, who began speaking fluent Mediaeval French and recounting stories of life in the Cathar region of Languedoc-

Roussillon. Guirdham then made it his life's work to prove that she really had lived then and known those very people she'd mentioned. He did.

Incidentally, the historical novelist Hilary Mantel, whose *A Place of Greater Safety* can just as easily be classed as a thriller, has intimated the work wasn't solely based on research. That she did actually 'hear' Robespierre's voice while writing. Just as George Bernard Shaw felt Jeanne d'Arc guided his pen while he wrote the play, *St. Joan.* This is where things become interesting, and I'm not the only writer who regards the process of creating and peopling a 'fictional' world, as an almost psychic experience. A few years ago, a well-published writer phoned me in some distress because she couldn't 'kill off' one of her characters as her plot demanded. The character herself was refusing to play ball. This isn't an unusual phenomenon.

In the thriller with built-in horror, anything is possible, and the question of 'how dark dare you go' is readily answered by Thomas Harris's *Silence of the Lambs* featuring a creepy psychiatrist, serial killer and cannibal epitomizing an extreme take on this sub-genre. He's our archetypal bogey man. The wolf in sheep's clothing until he bares those pinked teeth. Harris's prequel, *Red Dragon* also takes us to places we'd rather not tread, so why have these thrillers sold in their millions? Because they're daring and original. And after seeing Hitchcock's horror thriller film, *Psycho*, I wasn't the only one fearful of taking a shower for some time afterwards...

Anthony Shaffer's chiller, *The Wicker Man*, later filmed in 1973 starring Edward Woodward, is a cult classic, where the puritanical Police Sergeant Howie is lured to a remote Scottish island and a terrible end. The plot is outlined in Chapter 12. Its vivid and disturbing precursor, *Ritual*, by actor David Pinner, pits Christian Puritanism against Paganism to horrific effect in a small Cornish village.

Psychological thrillers also remain hugely popular. Sarah

Rayne and Nicci French both have strong followings amongst both sexes. Rayne's chilling *Tower of Silence* was inspired after she'd read a newspaper article on Indian death ceremonies, while French's *Killing Me Softly* involves Alice Loudon, a successful career girl in London who becomes hooked into the life of a duplicitous, manipulative mountaineer. Both are suspenseful examples of this sub-genre. There are many more, penned mainly by women.

In all the best thrillers, the reader is unsure whom to trust until the very end. In Gillian Flynn's best-selling second thriller *Gone Girl*, we're asking 'is it the husband or his wife who's telling the truth?' In my *A Night With No Stars*, which of the two brothers really killed their over-possessive mother?

A recent and gripping example of the literary thriller is Andrew Pyper's *The Demonologist*, where on a trip to Venice with his young daughter, Professor David Ullmann, a leading authority on demonic literature, hears the last words his late father ever spoke to him. From here begins an unforgettable journey into the deepest darkness in which he questions his beliefs. Shades of *Don't Look Now*, but different and daring enough to be published.

By your chiller thriller's end, too, the protagonist should have been irrevocably changed by events. Again, in *A Night With No Stars*, my optimistic protagonist Lucy Mitchell will never let herself be so gullible. In *Prey Silence*, Tom Wardle-Smith realizes after his nightmare in SW France, that 'east, west, home is best.'

Your thriller must also maintain momentum. Too much description, back-story and introspection will slow it up, yet to avoid a shallow read, all are needed in moderation and in context.

Each chapter in this book is deliberately structured – akin to the brick-building process – to help you construct a memorable chiller thriller in the form of a novel. I'll be including references to and relevant examples from my own books and other chiller thriller writers whose work has stirred me. I'll also sharing my personal experiences in the roller-coaster world of publishing, as a regular adjudicator of writing competitions, manuscript mentor and creative writing tutor, to encourage bravery. Why? Because I'm convinced that ultimately, agents and publishers don't know what they want until they see it. If you don't believe me, read how Mark Z. Danielewski's mind-blowing *House of Leaves* came into being.

Chapter 1

My Twelve Commandments

Crime/thriller writer Graham Hurley's simple dictum, 'be honest with yourself,' is true because you need to query, 'why do I want to write this? What makes it worth all the effort? What do I care about?' He then adds that nothing good happens without passion. Nothing excellent by passion alone. Thank you, Graham.

1   Action first. Explanations later.

2   Your protagonist must be really up against it.

3   Give him/her the initiative.

4   What do they stand to lose?

5   To gain?

6   Have a time limit. Then cut it to keep up the pace.

7   You'll be sharing your life with your characters so make them real. If they bore you, they'll soon bore the reader.

8   Know where you're going before you begin.

9   Always ask yourself, 'what's next?' Keep up the suspense.

10 Are you on the edge of your seat while you write? If not, take another look.

11 How have your main protagonists changed by the end?

12   Was it hard for you to let go at the end, or were you glad
     to be rid?

If hard, it may pay to consider a sequel, trilogy, quartet or longer
series. Keep this possibility on the back burner.

Chapter 2

I Won't Have The Time!

I can actually hear you say this, but don't panic. Everyone who's attended my writing workshops over the years, either held busy jobs, were studying in Higher Education, etc; juggling complex family situations with the myriad other time-consuming paraphernalia called 'life.' Yet all somehow managed to bring in recent work to be discussed and critiqued. All felt that without clinging on to what they felt to be their most important activity, their lives would have held less meaning.

When, in 1996 I had to leave rural west Wales for urban Northampton, I was bereft. No mountains, no unspoilt rivers, no real wildness, but in joining a writers' group under the aegis of Leicester University and led by an encouraging tutor, I connected with this gritty resolve, overcame my despair, and finally completed *Wringland*. I continue to be humbled by the circumstances in which aspiring writers find themselves, yet still cling to their dream of improving enough to become published. By honing their craft, by reading, and an inner determination, they will, whether by a mainstream or independent publisher or self-publishing in print and e-book formats. I would however, not recommend giving up your job or studying in order to write full-time. This not only adds unnecessary pressure, but removes you from relationships and situations which however difficult, do add to your experience store.

Also, in your covering letter to an agent or editor, an interesting or unusual job or qualification can add to your marketability. Although not a thriller writer, part of Magnus Mills' appeal lay in the fact he was a bus driver. Michael Ridpath worked in finance in the City when his best-selling financial thriller, *Free to Trade* was taken on. Another published author was a hospital porter who even wrote in longhand in the corridors. He was picked from the slush pile. Matthew Dunn, a former SIS member, uses this experience to great effect in his successful Spycatcher series.

As for myself, I taught art, ceramics and French in secondary schools for many years, which I considered, and still do, to have been a privilege.

"What are you writing now, Miss?" would often come up during lunch breaks in my art room, and animated discussion would follow. What should my characters do next? Who should meet a sticky end? I don't know if this helped with any GCSE results, but bonds were forged which later on saw these loyal pupils buying these very same books and keeping in touch with me about their own lives. Because of them and their unique lives, inspiration was never far away.

Many established writers claim in blogs and interviews that they write solidly all day and most of the night, but please take that with a big pinch of salt. Unless you banish your kids to boarding school and actually write away from home where the roof needs attention, the cooker's gone bust and the grass keeps growing. I admit that even in these days of 'gender equality, it's harder for women with growing families to quash feelings of guilt at the 'self-indulgence' of writing. Yes, I've heard that one many times, and it makes me angry. In her fine essay, 'A Room of One's Own,' Virginia Woolf was right. If Shakespeare had been female, things might indeed have turned out differently.

Time isn't the only issue. It's important to have some physical space of your own. You may well be able to think about possible characters and themes whilst multi-tasking, but there comes a point where bringing it all to life whether on your computer or longhand, needs that sanctuary. My small study's walls are covered with images that I've either drawn upon or might still do, and my computer is framed by photographs of my latest locations. Such a personal space doesn't need to cost you an arm and a leg. I've heard of one determined author who even locked herself in her car and sat in the back seat to write. Necessity certainly the mother of invention there!

Having won an international short story competition and been approached by an agent to write a novel, I bought an old caravan to put in our field. This became my writing home, and after marking a mountain of homework and making tea for our two daughters, this was 'the birthing room.' Although our large Beulah Speckleface sheep would sometimes share it! This first novel, *The Fold*, is an historical/paranormal thriller, now undergoing a brutal re-edit. Based on my many experiences of taking school pupils abroad, it's set both in Essex and a secretive area of southern France where these charges become more unruly until, in a frightening time-slip involving the Tower of Justice in Carcassonne, just one lucky lad, wearing his crucifix, is pushed out into the sunshine and safety.

Some writers need to work surrounded by sound. Sarah Rayne, author of engrossing psychological and historical thrillers, writes while listening to Mozart. I need silence, but then everyone is different.

You might add about yourself, "I've not written anything imaginative since I was a teenager. It all seems so daunting, and yet, I really do want to give it a go."

So, what's stopping you?

Exercises

i) Think back to what you used to write when young, whether in response to a teacher's given subject; something seen or heard, or your own creation entirely.

ii) Did you pen scary stories of murder, ghosts and vampires? Weird creatures taking over the world? Or what? Try and jot down a few memories. Do they fit any particular genre? Did you create a main character who still stays in your mind?

When I was eleven, my Dutch uncle took me to the Gröningen Museum in Bruges, where I saw in close-up certain diptychs and triptychs of the Flemish School in all their gruesome, surrealist glory. Here, the flaying of a cruel judge. There, a luckless criminal tied to four horses galloping away from him in four different directions. A hideous punishment. A nightmare narrative in oil paint on wood, revealing man's darkest capabilities that still subconsciously haunts my writing.

iii) Set aside a quiet twenty minutes, with pen and notepad/tablet etc. Select one particular object nearby to study in detail, from your point of view. Take 10 minutes to include the following in your writing. (Grab a Thesaurus if necessary to check out names of colours etc. There's more to just 'red' than red! The downside is, it's often hard to stop reading.)

iv) What is this object made from?

v) Its condition?

vi) Where did it come from?

vii) What does it represent to you?

Take a further ten minutes to; (in the past or present tense.)

i) Describe a different item from another character's point of view and in quite a different setting. Even another era. Also take their age into account. They could be quite young...

ii) Where exactly is this object?

iii) It seems curious/unsettling to the observer. Why might that be?

iv) What happens next?

And so, you have a small ball rolling into hopefully chilling territory!

Chapter 3

With a B.A here, an M.A there...

Should I bother?

While studying sculpture both in Manchester and at St.Martin's in London, I felt pressurised into having to please my tutors. One wanted me to produce Henry Moore lookalikes, (as he himself did, very ably,) and another, to copy the trendiest trends of what was becoming conceptual art. But I wanted to sculpt horses, and in the end, the tutors left me alone. I became a successful commissioned artist and exhibitor because my heart and passion lay behind my efforts.

As for my chiller thriller writing which developed later, I'm fortunate in that my influences remain what I dream, experience, observe and imagine. I'm also fortunate to be able to write what I want.

Having said all this, Degree and Post-graduate Creative writing courses can be fun and supportive and the best ones provide long-lasting contacts including useful ones within the publishing world. There are however caveats. They are big money-spinners flooding the literary scene with hopeful writers who may have been better off taking a job in the real world. The tutors may not have been published for a while and yet enjoy the power and influence they wield.

I did hear of a well-known agent who would rarely look at such submissions, claiming they were generally formulaic and very recognisably from certain institutions. So, how to weigh up what's best for you? To resist peer and glossy marketing pressure and climb on board your very own adventure bus? If you do decide upon either a full-time degree course or part-time Post-Graduate course, then there several important factors to consider.

Exercises

i) Using the internet, check out 4 possible courses in different locations. Nowadays, with fees, travelling/ living costs, I'd start with what's available closest to home. If home isn't an option, then either try an online course, or spread your wings. If you're a first degree student, there may be grants available that relate to your individual circumstances.

ii) Take a look at the staff involved. What's their publishing/research record? Check out their individual websites/blogs/Twitter etc. to discover what makes them tick. If you know that ultimately, you want to write genre fiction and they are all literary, then look elsewhere.

iii) Are there any examples of current students' work published in-house? If so, where does the emphasis seem to lie? On literary fiction and short stories? Or poetry?

iv) What are the opportunities for the next stage? E.g., the University of East Anglia awards the Curtis Brown Prize for their most promising MA Prose Fiction student. Some courses end with a professionally published anthology which may have a well-known author's introduction. This can be a useful first step on your writing ladder.

Other alternatives to a Higher Education commitment may be to enroll on one of the many Arvon courses (where bursaries are available) or Ty Nwydd in Gwynedd. Both last for a week and are considered to be excellent. Any good writing magazine will also give details of writing courses held abroad. For shorter breaks, try Urban Writers Retreats.

If your commitments and/or finances preclude the above suggestions, why not try joining a local writing group?

There'll be variations in quality and organization, however, as both an experienced tutor and participant, I believe they offer both the beginner and more experienced writer, inspiration, support and of course, useful feedback on their work.

I'd certainly have struggled to complete *Wringland* without Barrack Road Writers in Northampton, and its encouraging and talented tutor, Richard Foreman. Here in Wales, I belong to the wonderful Llanelli Writers' Circle which meets monthly and is another source of inspiration. The National Association of Writers' Groups (NAWG) hold annual competitions and a conference. Contact them or your local library to see if there's a group near you. If not, you can always join as an Associate Member.

Chapter 4

Who Am I?

Navel-gazing with a purpose.

Identifying your own and others' qualities and failings will help give your created characters greater realism and believability, whether dead or alive. People whom we perceive to be perfect, to 'have it all' may be far from it. Human beings are clever at keeping secrets buried, and, as a potential chiller thriller writer, it's important to feel the need and curiosity to unravel them. Alan Furst, a great spy thriller writer from the USA, claims that a degree in anthropology rather than English, is of more use to the fiction writer. How often, in a boring queue, do you listen to and observe those around you and ask yourself – for example - if the tattooed and studded guy in Asda would jump in the river and save you if your boat was sinking? Or is he about to pull out a hand grenade? As a writer, you won't be missing a trick and your unique imagination, like any other muscle in your body, needs using. Empathy and being able to relate to other people's lives is also essential. To be able to reel your readers into your characters' worlds which are more heightened and exciting than theirs is key. If they don't care about them, they'll stop reading. If *you're* bored and detached, you won't even get that far.

Exercises

i) Sum up in approximately 50 words, your own character, including good and bad traits. Be honest! Now be more specific...

ii) How do I react in a crisis?

iii) Am I sympathetic? A good listener? Do people confide in me?

iv) Do you envy anyone? If so, why?

v) Am I too curious? Has it got me into trouble?

vi) Have I betrayed anyone? If so, why?

vii) Has anyone betrayed me? How did it feel?

viii) Give 3 examples of a) My greatest joys. b) Deepest fears. 'Silence, is my deepest fear,' confessed one of my workshop writers, to everyone's surprise, and on page 7 of Suzanne Ruthven's , chiller *Whittlewood*, the ears of a London journalist arriving in rural Northamptonshire, 'could not come to terms with the awful silence.'

Several admitted that 'the countryside' unsettled them, and who can forget Rupert Bear who's either being pursued or observed by someone lurking behind a nearby bush?

Most respondents however, cite being buried alive as their deepest fear. Why else does novel and film, *The Vanishing* still exert such terror?

ix) What is the most frightening thing that's happened to me? (At any age.)

x) No man is an island. Who, close to me has caused me pain? Anxiety? (Even, as Tennyson so accurately wrote, 'little lacerations of the spirit?) Why? Describe this person/people.

xi) Who has brought me happiness and/or peace? (Whether briefly or long-term)
In what way? Describe them.

xii) What makes me angry/upset?

xiii) Am I rebellious or conforming? Why?

xiv) What secret/s am I still keeping? Why?

Examples

a) The Dutch *noir* thriller writer, chess player and cyclist, Tim Krabbé, author of the unforgettable *The Vanishing* and *The Cave*, also *The Rider* and *Delay*, is reluctant to talk about his background and yet it's hard to believe these bleak scenarios come from merely a ripe imagination. He has however, admitted how suffering always appealed to him. How cycling epitomises this, and as a youngster, he'd run tirelessly against his friends, aware he was able to endure great physical strain.

Here then, is a fascinating real-life character who might repay further study.

The following three excerpts show three fictional characters who present a normal persona to those who don't know what they conceal.

b) From the skillfully layered psychological and part-historical thriller, *Spider Light* by Sarah Rayne, where the mysterious Antonia Gray is driving to Charity Cottage. But who is Richard that she refers to, and why does she begin to feel uneasy?

She stopped mid-journey to top up with petrol and have a cup of tea – it was annoying to find that it took ten minutes to talk herself into leaving the safety of the car to enter the big motorway service station. But I'll master this wretched thing, said Antonia silently, I *will*. I'll turn on the car radio for the rest of the journey or put on some music – yes, that's a good idea.

Before starting off again she rummaged the glove compartment for a tape. There was a bad moment when she realised that some of Richard's favourite tapes were still here, but she pushed these determinedly to the back and sorted through the others to find something sane and soothing. There was some old pop stuff, which would be lively but which might remind her too much of the past. Was it Noel Coward who had said, 'Strange how potent cheap music is?' Ah, here was Beethoven's *Pastoral Symphony*. Exactly right. Hay-making and merry peasants and whatnot. Beethoven had just reached the Shepherd Song and Antonia thought she was about forty miles short of her desti-nation, when a vague half-suspicion began to tap against her mind and send a faint trickle of fear down her spine. She was being followed.

c) From my noir thriller, *Malediction*, in which Father Jean-Baptiste aka Robert Vidal who feels his Neo-Nazism and terrorist activities are justified, discovers his much-respected colleague Jacques Moussac is mysteriously dying. It's a pity Vidal doesn't also care enough for the brave woman who loves him, or the intended victims of his bomb. Yet this lover of Pérotin's church music is a hard-working priest, dedicated choir master, is here showing a tender side until he realizes that an incriminating letter about him is missing. Some readers actually rooted for his survival, blaming his family background for his wickedness.

No gate, so he vaulted over the fence and using the shrubs as cover, crept close to the French windows which opened out on to a small terrace. Immediately, the smell of sickness reached him and the sound of coughing in a tortured sequence racked the quietude. Moussac was there in that room, he could tell.

"Jacques?"

"Who's that? Robert?"

"What the Hell's going on?"

"Hell is correct. But you must go. I mustn't see you. It will only make things worse."

Vidal crouched low in case that girl should re-appear. The room faced north, its corners secretive, but he could just make out a Bechstein whose lid was closed and the draped bed end over a *pot de chambre*,

"Christ, Jacques, you were fine when I left to see my father."

"That was a lie Robert. You were sent to Villerscourt and thanks to Toussirot, I know the real reason why. Nothing to do with our choir... "

Vidal fell silent. So everybody knew his shame. That explained things.

Merci, Toussirot, you shrivelled old con.

The blonde girl came in, slopping fresh water and tried to close the windows but Vidal blocked her way.

"He's got to rest, can't you see?" She snarled a different mouth this time. A hardness that could never in all eternity have been Colette. He watched how she spilled some of the water and made no effort to wipe it up.

"Jacques, we've things to do," urged Vidal. "The Beata Viscera for Paris, the Alleluia Nativitas recording. Pérotin is waiting... "Already the familiar chords, the pulsing harmonies were playing in his mind.

"Not *we* my friend. You. I'm done for."

Vidal charged inside the French windows and lay across Moussac's body as the girl disappeared.

"For God's sake, what's the matter?" He yelled. "Toussirot? Is he aware of any of this? Is anyone doing anything?"

"Oh indeed. Much has already been done."

With a huge effort the fifty-nine year old turned over to face him and Vidal let out a cry seeing the sunken yellowed face that he hardly recognised. Not his eyes surely, once full of joy and purpose, now expressionless? A dribble of something vile slipped from the corner of his mouth and Vidal's stomach turned over.

"Oh Sancta Maria" He whispered, taking his cold hand. "Sancta Maria."

"I would like Confession." Moussac moaned suddenly. "Now." He strained to change his position, and his assistant knelt alongside, his crucifix resting on the other man's fingers.

"Glorious Holy Spirit, give me the grace to know all my sins and to loathe them... " Moussac faltered. "I greet you Marie, I greet you... "

Vidal gently wiped his chin. The stuff was like yoghurt. It was *he* who should be confessing, but he listened nevertheless and heard only the workings of his own mind. The doubts and disobediences. "Have you wished ill to those close to you?" he asked.

"I have no living relatives as you know but I have been a Judas to someone who is now very close."

Vidal moved nearer the rancid breath for every syllable.

What's he talking about?

"Your lover's son, he told me everything. He hated you, you know, but had no-one else to turn to."

"Go on." Vidal slowly, dreading what would come next.

"He also gave me a letter." Moussac's eyes closed as though the memory needed darkness. Vidal could hear his own heart loud and fearful. "I told him he should never have stolen from your house... "

"What do you mean, stolen?" Vidal shouted. "What letter?"

"A strange thing it was. No signature as I recall, just OPÉRATION JUDAS at the top, and a mobile phone number to contact. It was a personalised invitation to join the ACJ. To you, Robert."

d) The first part of my work in progress, a psychological thriller with a so-far unnamed narrator, who presents himself as a caring uncle...

PARADISE WOODS

There aren't many compensations to being laid off, especially now, with house repossessions growing like those bloody mushrooms over in Paradise Woods. I'm lucky my redundancy dough paid off the loan on my flat, so there's only basic stuff to worry about. Oh, and Joel. My nephew.

Ten, he is and a right little bugger. But it's my sister's fault, not his. The way she dumps him at school first thing for Breakfast Club until Homework Club. No wonder he prefers being round me in the holidays. Mending a puncture on my bike is more inter-esting than those TV cartoons meant for retards. I kid you not, she left him on his own once with a mobile and bumper pack of Wotsits on his lap. I should have shopped her, but he might have gone into care. Least I can give the poor little sod some kind of life as they're only up the street.

So here we are. A mid-week holiday treat for me as well, don't forget.

The aquarium's only been opened a month but already they're offering two tickets for the price of one. Too much bloody water all summer, if you ask me, but when Leanne said I could bring Joel along, I felt a real spring in my step. Why? 'Cos the lad was about to see stuff that might change his view on life altogether.

* * *

The darkness hits you first. Then the smell, like my gran's knickers left out for the wash. Colder than I'd expected, but Joel's hand feels warm in mine.

"This way," he yanks me along the slippery tiles. "Look! An octopus!"

We stop at the first glass box, lit only by a green light coming from a rock at the back. Eight slimy legs shimmy along the glass, but why no eyes? Seems a pretty thin display for the money, till I spot another, smaller octopus creeping up on the other from behind that same rock. Soon there's action. A fight or some mating ritual. Whatever, I'm not sure I want the lad seeing it. He's only ten after all.

I realize my right hand is empty.

"Joel?" But instead of his eager face, his damp brown hair and his red anorak, there's nothing.

Chapter 5

What's My Story?

A highly thought-of fiction editor once claimed she only read biographies. I can appreciate why. No-one's life is without interest, and many successful thriller writers subliminally draw upon their own, heightening remembered realities for greater effect. So, how about you?

Exercises

Jot down the following;

i) Where do I come from?

ii) Who are/were my parent/s, guardian/s, other?

iii) Draw a simple family tree connecting me to my family or other support group.

iv) What was my education?

v) What particularly interested me then? Why? Was it due to a family member? A teacher/tutor/professor? A chance meeting/conversation?

vi) Has my education/or lack of, left any legacies? If so, of what? E.g., a loathing of maths/an obsession with saints from studying a Theology degree/a desire to make up for lost time and learn about the Incas.

vii) Connect any 4 names on my family tree to places I have either visited or known well.

viii) Write a detailed, descriptive account of any 2 of these places (these can include interiors) that have played and may still do, an important part in my life.

(I really must stop using the big, dark kitchen that terrified me as a child, whenever we visited my Dutch grandparents' house on the Blorenge near Abergavenny.

Here, whenever their dog bit 'the char,' she'd bite him back!)

ix) Ask yourself, what emotions did I feel while writing about these places? E.g., Sadness, loss, pleasure...

x) Study at least 6 full obituaries either online or in the broadsheets. Trace the deceased's journeys through their lives. It's always fascinating to contrast beginnings with ends.

E.g., A grandmother born in Preston then orphaned, later moved to Iceland to study volcanoes.

All grist to the mill of surprises.

Examples

a) From my chiller, *Cold Remains* where we meet out of work art student and reluctant cook, Helen Jenkins in the kitchen at Heron House. She'd followed her heart by doing her Art degree at university, but in a recession, opportunities are slim. Anxious to please her dominating mother, she's taken this job, but still dreams of one day being a professional artist. However, little does she know what and who will stand in her way.

Wednesday 1st April 2009 12.10 pm.

In Heron House's gloomy kitchen, twenty two year-old Helen Myfanwy Jenkins used the heel of her hand to press down the pile of corned beef sandwiches that she'd just made, and immediately her mind hurtled back to her days and nights in Stanley Terrace below Aberystwyth University's colonnaded presence. Seat of her dreams for three years where no money and a lurking, unpaid loan limited her diet to whatever she could place between two slices of Tesco's Value white sliced bread.

Then, such restrictions hadn't mattered. Art was her life; part of her soul, so as long as her pulse kept going, she wasn't that fussed about what ended up on her plate. Her friends, especially Heffy (Hefina) Morris existed on Marlboro Lights and Cadbury's

Flakes. Others, on pot, bought and sold at the Vulcan Arms every Friday night. There'd only been one crackhead in her year and he'd drowned after leaping from the pier the day the Degree shows opened. "My exhibition," Rhys Maddox had written on a note left on his bedsit's pillow. "Worth a Distinction, eh?"

As she wrapped the neat column in cling-film to keep it fresh for Mr Flynn's lunch when he got back from the pub, she wondered what that intense idealist would make of her now. Here in the middle of bloody nowhere, on pants pay, while her precious oils, acrylics and canvases had lain untouched for over a month. Having interviewed a girl from a nearby home for adults with learning difficulties, plus twelve other candidates, he'd offered her the job. She'd then naively flung her arms around his neck.

That had been a February morning of blue sky and scudding clouds - the kind no artist would get away with. And now look. Beyond the kitchen's two rattling sash windows, a gale rocked the budding crowns of oak and the dead chestnuts into a mad dance. If this storm kept on into the night, as they often did, the longest branches would reach over to knock against her wall. Bang, bang... Worse was when Mrs Davies - or 'Gwenno' as Mr Flynn more familiarly called her - hovered around like a stick insect, appearing from some shady corner, stroking the same old riding crop she always carried, that tapered like a rodent's tail. Why Helen's preferred name for her was The Rat.

Another problem was the weather. It stayed the same for days, sometimes weeks on end. Quite different from near the sea where she could take her sketching easel outside and make a preparatory watercolor, knowing that for the finished work, the light, the colors would remain unchanged. But in her heart she knew that while she continued here at the gloomy rabbit warren called Heron House, any creativity was hypothetical. Her materials would stay unused; her ideas unexplored. If she had to explain why, she would say because of a growing feeling of entrapment. Of not fitting in.

b) In my part historical thriller, *Cloven,* thirty-two year-old Ivan Browning has had to leave London and a well-paid teaching post, after a tragic accident involving one of his pupils. It's not long before he realizes his move to the idyllic Tripps Cottage in rural south Northamptonshire, is doomed.

ONE

The VW Golf hit seventy. Too fast for an unmarked road, and Ivan Browning knew it, but not fast enough to get him through that bloody scary stretch between the two farms, Wiseman's and Small Copse, the latter charred and eyeless black against the sky like the unending hedgerow and the fifty oak trees he'd first counted out in the daylight.

That had been back in July – just after he'd moved from Islington into south Northamptonshire, and gratefully accepted his appointment as a Lifelong Learning tutor in pottery – when he'd done a practice run to Cold Firton village hall along that same three-mile stretch, when his car was lit between the trees' thick shadows by the high midsummer sun. Now, in late November, these same oaks hung pale and ghostly, their branches snaking white against the sunken moon, looming closer, hogging the windscreen it seemed, hogging his mind, until suddenly he saw double headlights veering round the bend in front of him.

He braked, heard the lurch of pots and all his other gear in the boot as he heaved his car halfway up on to the verge. His mind flashed back to that terrible night almost a year ago: a wet London street and a thirteen-year-old girl dying in his arms. After that he'd sworn never to drive again and yet here he was, facing fresh punishment, possibly death, as if what he'd endured since then hadn't been enough.

'Jesus. Shit.' His pulse was working overtime, thud-thud-thud in his neck. The lunatic was in either a Saab or a Vectra he first thought, but as the thing drew near Ivan could make out more clearly the bulk of a 4X4 taking up the whole width of the road. There was nowhere else for him to go. He was a sitting fucking duck. On impact, his wing mirror screeched from its moorings, then came a long butting graze along the sills which locked his seat belt tight.

Afterwards came a silent blackness, except for his racing heart, as the other vehicle's tail lights vanished. Ivan turned the ignition key, expecting to hear the familiar burr that would take him away from that deadly place, but the engine had died.

Suddenly – from nowhere – he sensed a wetness on his right hand. Not blood or sweat but the warm spittle of a mouth, leech-like, seemingly drawing out bit by bit the last dregs of his courage. Was it Vicky? Vicky Walker? For that had been the poor dead girl's name. In his mind he saw her face once more – her mouth twisted in a rictus of pain and terror. Those white lips moaning 'Mum? Dad? Where are you?' bringing her ebbing breath cold against his cheek, until there was nothing left.

He screamed inwardly, unlocked his seat belt with frantic fingers, then bailed out of the car. He could feel the long wet grass on his jeans, but it was the smell of the dead hare caught under the wheel arch which finally turned his stomach and made him run like a man possessed towards the first lights of Cold Firton village.

Chapter 6

Reading, Writing, Reading!

Whether you prefer reading from a printed book or on Kindle etc. find yourself an author hero to share your writing journey. You won't be copying, but instead be inspired. My own heroes are many and varied; Alan Furst's *The World at Night*, a stand-alone spy thriller set during WWII in Paris; Friedrich Dürrenmatt's *The Pledge* is a study of obsession in a claustrophobic Swiss setting, which was many years later, inexplicably filmed in the wide open spaces of Montana; Philippe Claudel's *Grey Souls* featuring an unreliable narrator in a bleak Northern France in 1917; Andrea Maria Schenkel's *The Murder Farm*, set in the aftermath of WWII, skewers the reader with its convincing multi-viewpoints, another unreliable narrator and the regular interspersion of an old ecclesiastical liturgy into the impending bloodbath.

Pierre Magnan's *The Murdered House* where the wind and rain of Provence lash your very mind, while Brian Moore's *The Statement* cunningly lures you into willing its ex-Nazi anti-hero to escape justice; Johan Theorin's time-layered, spooky *The Darkest Room* is the second in a planned quartet, all the more original for its wintry setting on a Swedish island full of myths and legends where loss and danger abound; Another island, the Isle of Lewis is Peter May's atmospheric setting for his present-day trilogy, while Robert Wilson's *A Small Death in Lisbon* is a fine, layered literary thriller beginning with an intriguing prologue. Adrian Magson's *Death on the Marais*, is the first in his series featuring Inspector Lucas Rocco in a rural backwater in 1963 Picardie where not all secrets from WWII lie buried. He creates vivid settings and his protagonist is refreshingly human but not overloaded with the usual problems. Peter Temple's *The*

Broken Shore, took me to Australia and I'm still there. All these, whether standalones or part of a series, are character-driven. What their protagonists do or don't do, propels the story. Keeps up the suspense. In the early stages of their book, some writers prefer creating a 'plot cage at the outset, within which their characters move to plan, leaving little room for maneuver. Some prefer 'writing on the wire' without a clue as to who's being summoned or what will happen at the end. Whatever method you choose, an early outline of the story can prove useful. (Please also see CH.10.)

Exercises

i) Name 3 novels/short stories in the chiller thriller genre that have gripped you. Why? Analysis will help with sustaining suspense your own work.

ii) Name any that disappointed. Why?

iii) Name 2 TV thrillers and 2 thriller films you've seen. What's your verdict?

iv) Watch the film/DVD of *The Others* – a supernatural chiller set initially in 1945 in an old house on a remote, unnamed island somewhere in the UK where a young mother and her children live in tense isolation until 3 mysterious servants arrive. Unease builds to panic and a shocking and memorable climax.

v) Note its structure. Were you caught napping? Could the clever twist inspire you?

The supernatural has always fascinated me, more so since experiencing several inexplicable and frightening events. The worst, in a brand new house which I later discovered, had been built on a mediaeval graveyard. It's no exaggeration to say that I almost died.

In response to reader interest in this sub-genre, publishers are now commissioning their top 'literary' authors to enter this previously murky world. Jeanette Winterson and Helen Dunmore, to name a few, have answered the call. Ten years after *Wringland* hit the shelves!

Examples

a) From my supernatural thriller, *Wringland* with its first diary entry in January 1841 by the vengeful Martha Robinson, and first page of Chapter One in 1996, where Abbie Parker, keen to start her job as a nearby housing development, meets the Reverend Peter Quinn. I hope this sets the grim tone of the book. Also the sense that here is an unseen force more powerful, more lasting than what's happening in contemporary Walsoken, Lincolnshire.

MARTHA'S STORY.

January 1841.

Even the birds are frozen on to the sky the way goose feathers stick to my coat. And cold so cold my fingers feel nothing. Ma Tully at the Dame School says another Ice Age is upon us and lets us keep our bonnets on. The one good thing this week. The worst is my draw scoop broke. It snapped like a Branta's neck and Mister Hemmings the gang leader says I will have to use my hands instead to clear Slaves Drain. I tell him God is looking down and sees everything, besides, as moeder says, he's just catchwork with no right to make us suffer...

ONE

"A stands for angel who praises the Lord.
B stands for Bible that preaches God's word.
C stands for Church to which righteous men go.
D stands for Devil, the cause of all woe."

Earth-coloured words in a warped black frame dated 1862. Abbie shivered in the half light, but there was more. Six sepia photographs, cracked and buckled like the wintry soil itself, each signed Gabriel Hemmings in a strong square hand. A litany of death without mercy, frozen in time.

She noticed, too, there were no men; just women and children, obviously all his workers, hoeing, twitching, piling bricks, their faces faded against the Fenland sky. Blurred to loam like all the dead Hicklings, Graylings, Saxons and Huguenots resting in their brief borrowed ground, their young hands white like the fronds of a Christmas pine.

Abbie pulled her denim jacket tight around herself, feeling their cold touch her own bones, wondering about the one little girl whose steady, almost defiant gaze met hers when suddenly a voice eddied through the gloom, destroying the moment.

"Is that you, my flower?"

Whoever had called out was coming closer from the darkness of the nave, moving the air, bringing an odd musty smell. Then she saw him: a tall cassocked figure looming in front of her, disappointment lengthening his face.

She recoiled, trying to judge how far she was from the door, then realised that it was impossible. She was trapped.

"I'm most awfully sorry," he composed himself, "I thought you might have been my factotum horticulturalist. Never mind, I expect she'll be along later. Meanwhile, welcome, my young friend." A smile stretched his lips, and Abbie was sure he could hear her heart. "Peter Quinn. Reverend. Pleased to meet you." A hand extended, marbled like a map, while eyes that swam in their sockets, trawled from her brown bobbed hair to her feet.

"I'm not stopping." Abbie inched away from his waiting fingers.

"Ah, but I could see you were finding these remnants of local history quite riveting. All people of our parish here, you know. And if old Samuel Scott, God rest his soul, of Rievely Hall hadn't been such a Good Samaritan, their fate might have been quite different." Abbie shivered again. "My dear, do you know there used to be a small school held in the chapel which he personally funded?"

"No I didn't." She needed to be out beyond the sliver of daylight that edged the door. Away from the catacomb smell and the creepy smile that hid the man's teeth.

"Mind you, not all the poor had the good fortune to be educated. Only those truly committed to the Lord... Would you like to come and see?"

"I've got an appointment, actually."

But he ignored her lie, his nose now just a millimetre from the tallest figure dressed in black in the first picture.

"'Martha Robinson who now lies cold, possessed a gift worth more than gold.' What d'you think that meant?" Quinn turned for their eyes to meet, and with a shudder she noticed the red of each eye corner.

"Looks like she possessed precious little." Abbie tried to back away.

"Ah, that's where you're wrong, young lady. The strength of four men isn't given to everyone, least of all a woman. She was by far and away the best labourer on the estate, and..." His voice changed in a way she couldn't quite fathom, "the kind of mother we'd all like to have, until, that is, she strayed from the Lord's path..."

b) From my *Cold Remains* where Helen Jenkins brings Jason Robbins, newly arrived at Heron House, to the nearby disused lead mine where she'd previously imagined seeing something very strange.

"There's no sign of the mine manager's house," Helen continued. "And talk was that several workers and those living nearby became seriously ill from the smelting. That graveyard's probably full of them."

"You mean lead poisoning?"

She nodded, thinking again of Heron House's two elderly occupants. "Never mind blood poisoning, it can cause mental illness severe enough for people to be institutionalized, hidden away by their families. Or worse. Apparently Caravaggio became really violent as a result of lead in his oil paints."

Jason had obviously never heard of that sensual painter's name.

"So no compensation, then?"

"I honestly can't say."

"You should have seen the Health and Safety freaks we had at Woolies. If it moved, disinfect it."

She smiled. "There were also lung troubles from the tailings."

"Hello?"

"Dangerous dust."

"And what the hell is *that*?" He waved at a half overgrown cave-like opening set in the grass and surrounded by barbed wire and another danger notice.

"An adit. It leads to the Angred shaft."

"Adit? Never heard that word before. Do cavers and potholers come up here?"

Helen knew her second laugh was way too loud. Too out of place. He was staring at her as if she too, was mad. "If you go down one of these, forget it. Make a will first. When Mr Flynn had a go, he said it was like descending to a watery Hell. Really shook him up, it did. He saw animal bones and God knows what else, so perhaps some predator had used that shaft as a kind of store."

"Wish I'd not asked," said Jason, clearly not joking.

Just then, a different object caught her eye. To the right of the opening stood the same eerie phenomenon she'd spotted three days ago. Black, motionless as before. She realized now what it was now turned to face Dinas Hill opposite.

"Sssh," she hissed to Jason. "Look over there. Quick!"

He followed her pointing finger. "Why? It's just some old stone."

"No, it isn't. Can't you see, it's the figure of a man. Looks like he's in mourning clothes."

"If you say so." Jason sounded more than fed up. And, despite the cup cake, was probably starving.

"Is that the best you can do? I mean, this is freaky."

"Let's check it out, then. I can try taking a video again."

"No." She held him back with surprising force. "He's up here for a reason. He's obviously interested in this place and we mustn't interfere."

"With no coat? No umbrella? And if he *is* real, how come he's just appeared out of nowhere?"

"You're right." Yet she knew Jason was wrong. Could it be that whoever it was, had made a showing just for them, like for her on Wednesday? If so, why? "Let's just hang around a bit longer," she whispered. "All might be revealed."

Suddenly, before she could stop him, Jason cupped his hands round his mouth and hollered out "Yo there!"

Shit.

The effect of this din was immediate. The previously faceless figure turned their way. Despite Jason's closeness, Helen gasped in fear at that pallid, pained expression, and worse, as the young, brown-haired man himself began to move. Towards them.

Chapter 7

And The Theme That Stirs Your Heart Is?

I was often asked by my former agent, 'Can you identify your market?' Well, I couldn't. It's all very well knowing that a lot of kids and teens enjoy playing war games on their Xboxes etc. or that most fiction readers are women and that those of a certain age who live in Dorset, enjoy romance and 'cozy' crime, but I've always believed that *I* was the market; the reader whom *I* had to please, and let's face it, it'll be *you* who must put in the passion and commitment to pushing out 80,000+ words.

And not every thriller writer wants to take on an apocalyptical view of this world or any other, as in Cormac McCarthy's *The Road* or the hugely successful *The Hunger Games*. Or to unravel the dark deeds of governments and various dastardly covert organizations. But current news over what exactly is entering the food chain is a dream of a theme, where even the 'Mafia' word has been mentioned. Could contaminated meat be part of some sinister ruse to wipe out Europe's poor and save countries billions in benefit payments? Who dares to go there? Never mind global issues, dramas played out between the walls of a home or work place or holiday venue of whatever era, can escalate to an equally frightening degree, where the past invades the present. Where madness reigns.

The future too, as in *Looper*, a recent TV thriller in which a man can earn a living by shooting those sent back from a further future, using time travel. Now that *is* a fascinating scenario. As is Lauren Beukes's *The Shining Girls* and Kate Atkinson's literary thriller *Life after Life*. However, just remember that a cast of four can be equally memorable as a cast of forty. One literary agent I spoke to considers 6 characters to be the maximum. However, your over-arching THEME should strive to be as original as possible, exploring our darkest hearts. The psychopath, the sociopath. The smooth but deadly operator. The reality that even an innocent-looking youngster can wreak havoc. Look no further than school and college mass killings in America, while *Orphan* explores how a mere child is capable of the deepest evil.

Your chosen theme may in part spring from what you have just written in these previous exercises. E.g., if your main interest lies with Mediaeval France, then this will be an area hard to ignore. An 800 year-old secret manuscript from mediaeval Iceland has clearly moved Michael Ridpath to pen his latest thriller, *Where The Shadows Lie*, set amongst a wild, volcanic landscape. If you love horse racing, this same spur may apply. What happened to Derby-winning Shergar remains a mystery. Or biology, with all its ground-breaking developments in genetics and medical procedures, or astronomy where space travel will soon be the norm, and zero gravity causes our muscle to atrophy and bones to fracture. All fascinating material for the futurist chiller thriller writer.

As for rebels, Galileo was a threat to the establishment, and such a loose cannon was be considered dangerous and had, like Jeanne d'Arc, to be stopped. They won't be the last, and expert art restorers, archivists, archaeologists - you name them - all add grist to a chiller thriller writer's mill.

Former mountaineer, Peter Hoeg wrote *Miss Smilla's Feeling For Snow*. Its striking title and unique snow-expert Smilla Jasperson who stumbles upon high-level secrecy and skull-duggery, make this an all-time great. Set in Greenland and published in translation in 1993, it's now being-re-printed. Brad Thor's *Black List* has another big theme. Where does ever-advancing technology leave our privacy laws? And what about the successor to drones - Cyborg-insects, developed to carry weapons. Even killer robots which will be in use by 2023? The *Scientific Reports* journal states that electrodes planted in a rat's brain enabled it to pass information to another rat thousands of miles away. Remote viewing has intrigued me for a long time, and I've brought this theme into my thriller *Office For The Dead*, still being edited.

You may be fascinated by cryogenics, robotics and the possibility of computer-stored souls. All there for the taking. And which unlikely character will devise a death clock which correlates our birth and death dates? And for those of us who've had blood transfusions, do we ever wonder whose blood we have? Indeed, if it's human...

Eco-chiller thrillers will always have popular appeal as this planet continues to be defiled and overburdened, but your theme should not only be as original as possible, but tap into our deepest fears. It's frightening to read of future water wars. Or battles over fishing on the high seas away from territorial waters where even now, cod supplies are dangerously low and the sea bed itself is being scoured to death. And how are billions of hungry mouths to be fed? Use your imagination! Hospital waste may soon be on the menu, and I'm not joking. One gynecologist admitted to feeding his hens on hysterectomies, so this is not as far-fetched an idea as it sounds.

Henning Mankell, creator of the complex Swedish detective Kurt Wallender, claims that today's writers should show ambition with their characterizations and make their books pertinent to the societies we live in.

Two very valid points.

And if you feel emboldened to deal with another era in the past or the future, and events of which you know nothing; of characters the polar opposite to yourself, give it a try. Whatever you decide, remember, the most convincing writing comes from the heart!

If you're excited, your readers will be too.

Moonyeen Blakey's wonderful historical thriller, *The Assassin's Wife* springs from her love of history. Her main character, young Nan can foretell the fates of the Princes in the Tower. But can she betray their killer?

Like settings, certain themes have already had a good innings. WW1 and WW11. People trafficking. The Eastern European sex trade. The bad side of Victorian London. The Troubles in Ireland. Trippers in Thailand. The Vatican and Opus Dei; Gangland and organized crime, although Robert Crais' new LAPD thriller, *Suspect*, does at least have an ex-IED sniffer dog, Maggie as co-protagonist.

While Dan Brown was accused of plagiarizing Henry Lincoln, Richard Baigent and Richard Leigh's *The Holy Blood and the Holy Grail* for his *Da Vinci Code*, his later *Angels and Demons* set in Rome, shows originality, strong motivations and a great setting. The tension ratcheting up with each gruesome, symbolic murder. His latest thriller, *Inferno*, inventively uses Dante's work as a portal to mystery. With the imminent election of a new Pope, the Relatio - two secret files compiled by three cardinal-detectives after documents were leaked by the then Pope's butler – will be studied closely. An unconfirmed report claims a gay sex ring existed in the Vatican, some of whose members were black-mailed.

Unless, however, you have a really new angle on things ecclesiastical and biblical, steer well clear. *The Moses this, The Jesus that* and Uncle Tom Cobley have run their course. So have the Templars and their Freemason followers.

Kate Mosse however, seems to have cornered the Cathar-loving market, with doorstoppers such as *Labyrinth, Sepulchre* and *Citadel*. She, like myself has a house in the Languedoc Roussillon region of France which clearly inspires her work. These historical thrillers are well researched, full of suspense and above all, readable.

UFOs and other phenomena continue to exert a grip on our collective psyche, and still remain gifts for the chiller thriller writer, particularly as it has taken our Ministry of Defense fifty-four long years to release secret papers ruling out their existence.

Again however, the crux is originality. ET has been done and remains unforgettable. However, who knows, you might create the next global sensation!

And don't forget our Royal family. There are people out there who truly believe it's they, not Elizabeth II who should be the monarch, and while horrors in the NHS continue to surface, one fearless emeritus professor in the care of the elderly, claims that the contentious and ubiquitous 'Liverpool Care Pathway' appears to have become a license to kill. Now there's a story…

Exercises

i) Recall at least 6 items of past and/or present national/international news still lurking in your mind. E.g., GM crops. International food contamination connected to the Mafia. Terrorism. Richard II's bones found under a Leicester car park. A political cover-up. A man still missing from a cross-Channel ferry…

ii) Write them down. Why do they still linger? Do you really believe what you've read/heard?

iii) Also write 4 possible themes for your thriller set fully/partially in the future.

iv) Write 4 other possible themes for exploration using the past and/or present. Or both. If you can't stop writing about one in particular, that's a good sign!

Animal welfare is another of my preoccupations. Over the years, we have rescued sheep, ponies and dogs. My regret is that we couldn't have done more, and when I and many others see gratuitous cruelty meted out to livestock in farms and slaughterhouses, we are shocked, but not as powerless as we once were. I have stood outside well known stores to protest at their factory farming conditions and have tried to persuade live animal transporter drivers at several British ports, to turn back. In *Prey Silence*, one of my main protagonists is the brutish Samson Bonneau who rears veal calves illegally. Natalie Musset, a fearless animal rights activist begins to investigate but soon puts herself in the greatest peril.

I had little idea how short and cruel are the lives of veal calves in unregulated countries. I do now.

Examples

a) There is a recurring theme to Tim Krabbé, the Dutch *noir* thriller writer's first three books. The reunion of two lovers in death. Darkness is Krabbé's trademark, suggesting a brooding, melancholic imagination. The seed for his unforgettable *The Vanishing*, filmed in 1993, apparently grew from a newspaper clipping, but he's reluctant to say what's in the well from which he draws this remarkably vivid fiction. The opening to this pivotal chiller thriller novel and film sees Rex's fiancée, Saskia vanishing from a French service station while he spends the rest of his life searching for her. Meanwhile, the 'respectable' teacher/sociopath Lemone goes free. Being buried alive is our most primal fear, but now added to that I make sure that every time we visit a French service station, our car doors stay locked! Seriously. Such is the power of ideas.

Krabbé tries to stay naïve about what's going on, and is only concerned with telling the story. That if it's good, the depth will come all by itself. Interestingly, aged thirteen, he'd also admitted being relieved by his parents' divorce.

b) In Michael Cordy's highly original thriller, *The Miracle Strain*, his theme centers on the sacred quest by an ancient, secret brotherhood to discover the genes of God. But they also need Dr. Tom Carter's knowledge and expertise. This Nobel prizewinner for Medicine is however, in Boston USA, still struggling to cope with his wife's murder in Stockholm, and seeking a miracle for his young daughter's incurable brain disorder.

c) Jean-Christophe Grangé's *Empire of the Wolves*, set in Paris and Turkey, in which a young woman goes to extremes to disguise her identity to avoid death in a ruthless drugs war. This is a brave and different thriller with a strong female protagonist.

d) In *Bloodstream*, my thriller set in the Vosges in 1975, sixteen year-old Pauline Archibald from a Manchester suburb has arrived at *Les Sapins* as an *au pair* to the Vincente's two older and unruly children. Where the youngest has mysteriously disappeared from the garden. I wanted to convey the claustrophobic area and her vulnerability to not only the pigs, but also to what might lie ahead...

CHAPTER ONE

The road, wide enough for only one car, left the smooth silent river Choiseuf at the point of its tightest convolution under the bridge, and followed the line of the hill up towards Millevaches. Hidden from grazing land and forestry by the high overgrown hedge, the English girl removed her hand knitted cardigan as she walked, and tied the sleeves into a cumbersome knot over the already burgeoning form ripening in harmony with other fruits of branch and briar bank. Umbelliferous clusters of raw green elderberries merged with catmint, nightshade and cow parsley, making a fetid barrier of early summer growth. A rare presence in that closely cultivated corner of Lorraine where borderless fields stretched eastwards to the Vosges foothills.

This hedge marked off Joseph Clissot's territory, lining the road and brushing against her white English legs. Far below, she could hear the Mediterranean "expresse" drawing its chain of crowded sun-seeking carriages through flat patchwork farmland, from grey and the threat of rain to guaranteed cerulean blue. Suddenly, a large black sow appeared rooting and snuffling in a wayward indecisive manner, coming her way, together with a troupe of well-grown weaners and yet more scavenging adults.

The girl pressed her back against the sticky bristling shoots of nature's wild abandon, not daring to breathe, watching their advance. A young boy, who despite his serious expression and ill-fitting dungarees, couldn't have been older than seven or eight, pursued his charges waving a forked stick. She'd never seen him before, this small guardian who in an instant could lose a limb if those porcine jaws so chose. Nevertheless, he circled around the leader forcing it to retreat snorting and defecating as it did so. The others jostled in its spattered wake, through to a high sloping field opposite the turning for St Gannat.

With a few deft movements he secured the gate and with her heartbeat still thudding in her ears, she wondered how many children in her Manchester suburb could have done the same. But weren't they all of a practical and resourceful nature in these parts, once chosen for a renewed German offensive in 1940? Bomb-blighted and hurriedly rebuilt by Armand Retiers, his farm was all that now remained of the tiny, inbred community.

In the silence that followed, she crept from her stifling sanctuary and looked around at this foreign landscape so different to the grey, bleak moors nearby where her mother would regularly march her along at a furious pace in the battle to lose weight. For a moment, this alternative seemed preferable, and she considered sneaking back to the sad *Les Sapins* then thumbing a lift back to the station. But something held her back. That photograph on the dining room sideboard of little Gérard-Louis Vincente. Still missing from home. His big brown eyes hypnotising her even here. Pleading to be found.

Chapter 8

I Must Be Mad...

No. Writing your chiller thriller will actually keep you sane. It could even save your life if everything else is going to hell in a handcart. Creating your own world is a wonderful, mysterious experience, so relish it. There's no need to panic. You can make your writing the most important part of your day, even if you're not actually writing.

Exercises

i) While you're driving, typing up a boring document, taking a shower, changing a nappy, walking wherever, try connecting up with what you've explored so far. Allow ideas to follow. It's useful to keep handy some means of recording these for later. I find that a notebook on the bedside table is invaluable for even just 5 precious minutes' of 'catching up' and jotting down possible next steps.

ii) Remember to keep your writer's 'antennae' on alert. Nothing is wasted. Not even your neighbor putting out his rubbish. Supposing it looks suspicious? Does he or she seem shifty?

iii) Take a look at *A Crime in the Neighbourhood* by Suzanne Berne, a 7 year-old girl is the narrator who, after a recent local murder, sees her male neighbor cooking on his barbecue while in the nude. The end is truly chilling and believable.

iv) Write down at least 3 things you've noticed about your own vicinity which have triggered your curiosity. Your fear. Even your rage.

Remember, nothing, however close to home, is wasted.

Chapter 9

Sowing Seeds

We're all human. The prospect of launching into a full length novel is, to even the most prolific and successful writer, a daunting one. Each attempt a massive undertaking. To help you bridge the seeming chasm between idea and end product, I'd ask you to consider writing a short story as a starting point – a toe in the water - to test if your chosen theme has 'legs' for a full-length chiller thriller. Word counts for short story submissions tend to fall between 2,000 – 5,000 words, although I have encountered a few under and over these limits.

A novella is another consideration. Generally around the 30,000 – 50,000 word count, there seem to be more of these books around, and I personally enjoy reading them because of their necessary conciseness. Friedrich Dürrenmatt's *The Pledge* is a prime example. Also, Taichi Yamada's *Strangers*, while *Eight German Novellas* is one of my favorite collections which includes Theodor Storm's haunting ghost story, *Pale Horse Rider*.

The short story, whether representing genre or literary fiction or the blurred space in between, also seems to be undergoing something of a revival, and certainly there are many reputable and valuable national and international competitions where the end result is not only prize money but inclusion in an anthology available in bookshops and/or online.

To win, be placed or Commended is an added bonus for your writing CV, and a strong showing in either the prestigious Bridport Prize, the Bristol Short Story competition, The Fish Short Story competition, the *Aesthetica* Creative Arts competition or *The New Writer* Prose and Poetry Prize to name a few out of many, many more, will raise your profile and could certainly swing an agent or editor into taking a punt on you.

Within the crime/thriller genres there are yet more opportunities, for submitting online or by post to either e-zines and/or printed magazines. *Ellory Queen Mystery* Magazine, *Spinetingler* magazine, etc. If you have internet access, you'll see numerous sites listed where short story submissions in the thriller genre are welcomed.

Sean Jeffery's *Dark Tales* quarterly anthologies definitely convey what's on the tin. Alarming visions by gifted writers. Although the bias is on Horror, many stories have the thriller's momentum.

I began writing short stories long before any novel came along, and I continue to use them as a kind of litmus paper. The testing of a particular theme. The surprise success of my *Magnum Opus* – a sci-fi/thriller hybrid – in an international competition, not only secured me an agent, but showed me that the bizarre idea of an impecunious student struggling to pick enough mushrooms in an underground mushroom farm amongst so many flickering lights and the choking stink of dried pigs' blood, could herself become one, was feasible.

Much later, in another short story chiller, *Friends in High Places,* set in a remote Scottish lighthouse during Victorian times, I again explored the theme of human metamorphosis. This was published in *The New Writer,* and helped validate my interest in what others might consider a far-fetched notion. So, thank you to its brave editor!

In 2008, bluechrome published my first short story collection, *Strangers Waiting.* Its eponymous title relates to my short story set in 1830 before cattle were transported across Britain by train, when a naïve young girl accompanies her uncle's drove from Wales to England. She survives his assault and other depredations, but when the drove stops near a country estate where all is dangerously not as it seems, her fate is sealed.

I'd researched how commonplace it was for such vulnerable youngsters to be taken in this way to the kitchens and gardens of

English stately homes. Imagine the outcry today. So this was exciting territory, and my second chiller *Cloven* was born from my explorations. This short story won the H.E. Bates Award for Short story.

The short story collection is available on Kindle.

Top agent, John Jarrold wisely says, "Know the parameters of the genre, but your own voice is so important."

Exercises

What seeds might *you* be ready to sow?

i)   Decide on a theme that you cannot ignore.

ii)   Write a 50 word outline for your short story...

iii) With no other distractions, close your eyes and try to picture the scene you're about to portray, with all senses on alert. It's as if you are a film director with a clear vision of what you want your audience to see and experience.

Examples

a) In *Clan*, from my published short story collection *Strangers Waiting*, student Fiona Carter works in a pub in a remote corner of Argyll. Here, in reality, grim myths and legends abound. Its history has been one of violent struggle. The locals inbred and hostile to incomers.

I visited the area a few times where the omnipresent moss was too brightly green. The gloomy forests too full of unseen dangers...

This complete short story is already forming the basis for a new chiller thriller, where a terrifying past rocks the present.

CLAN

The drizzle hadn't let up all day. Sly and silent in the growing dusk, it now permeated Fiona Carter's clothing, chilling her skin as she walked from Kilforgan's only pub to her small red hatchback in the overflow car park across the road.

"See ye tomorrow, then." Called a voice from behind her. She spun round to see Donald McKenzie's face filling the open attic window below The Wild Thistle's wet, dark roof. His smile like a black scar, his eyes too fixed on her for comfort. But what could she do? Her part-time barmaid's job was all she'd been able to find to help fund her English degree course at Glasgow university. The sole offer after her two other A level subjects had let her down. 'Options' was a word for other, luckier people. Not her.

She didn't answer him. It was enough that he chose the dire music tapes to fill her ears each afternoon until 8 pm. That he often passed too close to her in the pub's narrow passageways, stopping too long before moving on. If she complained to his dad who owned the place, she'd be given her cards and then what?

Fiona heard the window shut as she unlocked the Saxo. A basic model with no alarm or immobiliser. But then wasn't Argyll altogether safer than Northampton where car theft was rife? She kept the pub in her sights through the wing mirror while waiting for a suitable gap between the string of caravans and camper vans trundling towards Oban. Although it seemed little more than a harmless sugar cube, green-stained by years of damp, she knew better. That it was just a matter of time before she must risk her meagre income by handing in her notice.

A single-track lochside road now, with rare passing places and high mossy walls on either side, guarding the dense forests whose sawn firs heaped into house-sized stacks, bled sap from each cut.

Suddenly the lights of some huge oncoming lorry seared through the darkness ahead of her.

"Dammit."

Her wipers were too slow in clearing the film of viscous, yellow insect innards off her windscreen. Then came the wheeze of brakes, the rip of rubber on mud. She and the white-fronted Daf truck stayed face to face. Its grimacing radiator grille, the blinding headlights turned on full, all conspiring to rob her of a precious evening in her digs completing her English assignment for the start of the new term. Just then, her cosy room seemed to be on the other side of the world...

Whatever else Donald McKenzie had said about her, pushover she was not.

"I'm staying put," she told herself, reaching for her mobile. "This bastard's just ignored a passing place. I can see the sign." Besides, reversing had cost her two previous driving tests. No way was she attempting that risky manoeuvre here.

"Move, will you?" Came a female voice from the cab's open window. "I've fresh trout to deliver."

Fiona hesitated. Okay, so the driver wasn't a man. But why couldn't she place that familiar voice?

"I'm giving you ten frigging seconds. One... two..."

The other engine revved, bringing the beast closer. The impact forced the Saxo back, inch by inch while panic made Fiona unclick her seat belt.

"Stop!" She yelled, but was anyone listening? And, just as she was about to bail out, her rear wheels slewed from right to left, taking her off the narrow tarmac on to shingle.

"Jesus!"

But just as the loch's black water seemed to rise up behind her, came the juddering clash of steel against rock. She located the door's handle and her knee shoved it open, letting in the stench of dead fish. But she'd been lucky. A single boulder had stopped her slide into Loch Lomond where her Mum and Dad often brought her as a kid, until debt worries took him away forever.

Dad... Who'd chosen her name meaning 'white and fair' as a souvenir of happier times. But never since he'd locked himself in the bedroom of their Kingsthorpe home and turned on the gas fire, had she felt so powerless. Her mobile slipped from her lap on to shingle and vanished under the car.

Fearing the car's petrol tank might explode, she tried scrambling up the bank to the road and follow where that lorry had gone, but pain shooting down each leg from her hips meant she could only crawl. Next came the sound of feet running on stones which rattled like old teeth, and above the fish smell she detected something different. A woman's perfume. Sweet and equally repellent.

But it was the laugh which drove her to take cover behind a fallen tree trunk. A laugh soon joined by a male voice she knew only too well.

"You there, Fiona? Got your phone. Ha."

Panic.

How the hell had he known she was there? What to do now? She wanted her phone but not him or his unborn baby. Eight weeks ago it happened, and the moment her home-test kit said positive, she'd sorted a termination for next Thursday at a Glasgow clinic. Four days away.

He'd caught her by surprise on her first busy evening at the pub. Pressed her against the damp, bumpy wall near the boiler room before lifting her skirt. Then the rest, with his hand clamped on her mouth. Threatening her job if she blabbed...

"Our Marie's got a Rotty, remember?" McKenzie went on. "Not been fed for a while neither..."

Marie. Of *course*. His only sister. Five months gone, she'd boasted during their one recent conversation in the bar. Some fish farm worker it was, keen to marry her by Christmas. Fiona had seen the huge dog too. But why were the McKenzies after her? Nothing was making sense, except that she must distract them.

Nearby lay a sizeable stone and, with the greatest effort, she hefted it in the opposite direction along the bank.

"This way!" Donald McKenzie yelled to his sister. "Fuckin' move."

Fiona's tights were shredded at the knees. Her elbows' skin too, and by the time she'd scrambled up to the road, screened by the thickest trees ever, she could scarcely breathe. And then, through the dark drizzle, a spectral whiteness showed above the roadside wall. That same lorry tucked into a passing bay.

No time to wonder how she'd reach the driver's door handle let alone the cab, but she did. Or rather, it was her dead Dad taking her pain, making everything possible. She dared not slam the door but held it close as she started the engine and drove off single-handed, praying the road ahead would stay clear.

She couldn't see any other parked vehicle, so presumably Donald had been with his sister in the cab all along and they'd driven the long way round to meet her… That thought made her quicken along the twisting road, gritting her teeth to keep the stabbing pelvic pains at bay. Wherever those two were, they could soon be on her trail and being so conspicuous was a risk with the cops too. Not that she'd seen many, but from what she'd overheard in the bar, the McKenzie clan seemed to dominate this small corner of Argyll. Above the law too. Above suspicion. And another one growing inside her…

She had to lose the lorry fast and, as if her dad was helping again, a convenient forestry track led off on the left. Here she parked and struggled to the ground to get her bearings. More drizzle, stronger now and rustling sounds coming from the invisible plantation beyond the track. She hobbled towards the road, keeping as close to the stone wall as possible. Her ruined shoes sliding in the muddied ruts made by previously speeding vehicles. This way led back to Kilforgan and its pub, but at least she had coins for the callbox there to phone home. Like her digs, Spinney Hill seemed a world away. Her Mum already a stranger…

"Hello there, young lassie. Can I help you at all?"

Fiona stopped and in the darkness spotted an aged woman wearing a shawl over her head standing in the doorway of a tiny bothy shielded by a mass of trees. Not the first time had her powers of observation slipped. She, once the sparkiest girl in her school's mixed sixth form, was losing it.

"Would you be liking a nice cup of tea?" the old creature persevered. "I can see you're having trouble walking… " Fiona wondered why her colourless eyes were fixed on her stomach and instinctively pulled her shoulder bag round to conceal it.

Never mind tea. Vodka and Coke more like, she thought, unsettled by this woman's focus, aware of her own dry mouth. Her utter exhaustion. The offer of a drink now very tempting indeed.

"Thanks. And d'you happen to have a phone I could use?"

The woman nodded and, although no telegraph wires were visible, Fiona found herself drawn towards the dwelling. Her pain seemed to dissolve as the damp silence enveloped the past, the present unravelling in this realm of ash trees, tall as cathedrals where a deep eerie stillness she'd not experienced before, held her like a fly in amber.

She soon reached a tight gap in the wall and groped her way down the sloping overgrown path to an open front door. Here she stalled for a moment before stepping inside, only to find the old woman had gone. In her place, the sound of bubbling water; that same nauseous smell of dead fish, and sure enough in the gloomy kitchen on a table covered by a worn oilskin cloth lay three plump trout; blood lining their open mouths while six lifeless eyes stared at the flies circling above their speckled flesh.

Where could the crone possibly be? Had she been hallucinating?

"Now, me wee lassie," that same voice broke the silence. "Take a seat while I pour the tea…"

Fiona spun round, relieved to see her new acquaintance move towards the stove, her black skirt whispering against the stone flags with every step. Her face in close-up resembled an ancient rock hollowed by the tide. Fiona duly chose the nearest chair whose sagging weave cradled her sore hips while her hostess poured water from a buckled pan into a chipped brown teapot. She noticed the spent candles in sconces ranged along the walls, that the stone sink had no taps...

"You said you had a phone," she reminded her, watching the flies multiply.

"Did I indeed?"

"Just now. When I first met you."

The old woman filling two tin mugs with tea, was no longer an attraction. Escape was priority.

Then a shiver because the front door was now firmly shut with two black bolts drawn across. But why the sudden security? She'd not hear anything or anyone outside. Within two silent steps, the topmost bolt lay in her hand.

"No ye don't." That same body with its sour breath suddenly stood in the way, but when Fiona tried to push it aside, her fists met icy swirling air. Then a knife gripped by yellowed skeletal fingers, was pointing at her stomach.

"The McKenzies won't have no foreign blood taking their name. We fought long and hard here to keep you Sassenachs out..."

"What do you mean?" But in her deepest, trembling heart, Fiona knew.

"Marie, me great great grand-daughter told me. She can see things. She's got the gift... Their bairn's due near Christmas. Hers and Donald's. They don't want yours. None of us does."

Hers and Donald's?

"Let me go!"

Only the knife was real, solid, still pointing at her. Fiona backed away.

"I wasn't going to keep it anyway. I was raped. Ask Donald."

All at once, those two bolts began to slide aside of their own accord and the opened door revealed two figures framed by a mass of darkly swaying firs. The man with the black smile let the dog enter first, his jaws edged with spittle, clamped on a roll of Kilforgan Council bin liners.

b) This complete short story, *Strangers Waiting* became the forerunner to my thriller *Cloven*.

STRANGERS WAITING

The mist still lay low enough to seal all the penitent but imperfect souls close to the winter earth. Including herself, thought fifteen year old Eira Williams for her guilty pleasure in leaving the constraints of home.

Named after the snows that linger like shreds of sail cloth on Capel Ffin, she was now just as pale, just as frozen after a long day on the road, and let Fly, the head drover's dog, lick her face. He reeked of cow dung but no matter, with his tongue like hot bacon on her cheek and his ribby warmth enough to keep her from death, she gripped his collar as if he was the only rock back in the flooded river Bran.

All she could see were his two front paws, white as ladies' gloves. The rest so blurred that the girl come to work at Castle Ashby House in Northamptonshire couldn't see where her bed for the night and the coat she'd sleep in began.

That garment was her father's most prized possession, specially cleaned of straw for the morning the porthmon Moses Richards called to add her to his herd of Pembrokeshire Blacks strung out like lumps of coal along by Gallt y Mwyn, and impatient to be off.

"Don't ever be parted from it." Evan Williams warned. "The Saesneg will sell anything my girl."

"Oh Evan, don't." Pleaded Mrs. Williams. "It'll do her good to see the world and get fattened up with the rest of them. Won't it, cariad?"

Eira nodded, aware that Moses' twin kept his piggy eyes on her all the time.

"You forgotten about Non Jenkins then?" The farmer persisted, buttoning up his daughter with the best boars' teeth on the best 'brethyn cartref', rough on her throat but heavy as a shield against his fears, so she could at least smile a farewell to them both and wave once they'd merged into the drizzle.

But Eira heeded him nevertheless, and the coat stayed on her back for all of the next three weeks. Through Sennybridge and the joining with Llew Lewis's drove of Shorthorns. Though Aberhonddu, Hereford and places she couldn't pronounce, as west became east with the weather grown cold as prayers of the dying. However, those weren't the only changes.

By the time they'd reached Northamptonshire she knew Aaron Richards had a mind to make her his woman. She could tell the way he fixed on her and worked his tongue round his lips whenever she caught his eye. Twice she'd fought him off, and twice he'd returned for more. So now with night falling, Eira made sure she was settled well away from him and Gwallter Jones in the dark bank along Sulgrave Lane.

Suddenly a whistle and the dog leapt from her lap. Moses Richards was swearing that God must have dropped his guard and let Satan take his place.

"Those who blaspheme on All Souls will have their hearts bound with flax," she whispered, then sat bolt upright, her ears tuned to a blur of sound which gathered momentum like the workers' chants in the forestry.

But this was no singing.

"Haiptrw Ho!" Boomed through the mist, alerting her into the hedge. She clung to the pleached hawthorn as the panic swell grew closer, thundering down to the deep end of the world, choking the narrow lane with the Pembrokeshire Blacks in front taking low branches on their shoulders.

Then the Shorthorn bullocks sensing freedom, pressed the leaders up the banks until the way ahead was clear. Eira felt them on her coat and prayed aloud until it was the only sound in the curdling stench of blood and scouring. Next, out of the haze, boots pounding like a drum roll. Her voice locked in terror. They were leaving her behind. Even Aaron Richards. Even the dog.

Her teeth juddered in the silence as she slithered down the gulley. Ox blood hung in the air, stiffening on her coat. Suddenly a hand to end it all came stinking on to her face, flattening her nose.

"No need to call out, Miss Snow. Ye'll be all right now." The twin who'd crept back from the others tried to hold her close. This ugliest of God's works with the scurvy and breath worse than the pig floor at Nant y Ffin would never touch her again as long as she lived. "Better come with me if you want to get where you're intended." His nails reached her bones like the vermin traps up on the Moel Pregethwr. "We got them all in, thank the Lord. Went sweet as lambs at the end..."

Sweet as lambs.

Eira shivered, plotting furiously how best to escape. The only weapon was her voice, so she set her jaw and took in a great gulp of air. But Aaron Richard's hand was there again.

"Castle Ashby's two days from here. How'll you manage that?"

"I'm not going."

Just past Southam when his eyes had gone straight through her clothes she'd decided to find a return party to take her home. Capability Brown or no Capability Brown, she wasn't going to be a sitting duck in the pretty winter gardens just for his pleasure. She heaved and sicked up.

"Brwnt gast!"

The blow sent her to his feet, and once more in the darkness, Death's finger beckoned.

"Aaron?" His twin bellowed. "What you a doin' of? Jones and Lewis here's on their own!"

Eira sensed her captor's indecision. Subservient to his brother who by being married held the Drover's Licence - the upper hand, and on a night such as this, a warm bed. She took the advantage and ran up the lane as Moses' threats continued.

"At Maidford, I'll see you get nothing! And nothing means nothing!"

Her heart like a hammer, Eira waited for the man's next move, but only sighs of the long-dead reached her as she dodged lose stones, the strewn limbs of ash and beech and pools of dung.

At the crossroads to Moreton Pinkney the sign lay broken. Nor was there any moon or stars to set north or tell the time. Was it still night or dawn? Without birdsong who could say? Only those above it all whose vision lay unclouded by matter knew the answer. At least that's what The Wizard of Cwrt y Cadno had said when they'd called in for his rinderpest cure.

How she longed for their gift now, turning as though in a solitary game of Blind Man's Bluff, in a strange country with neither coin nor candle to her name. She thought of twp Non Jenkins from Siloh. Sold with the milk near Banbury and found on St. Swithin's day in two forage bags. Better she'd been taken by footpads - at least she'd have had a chance...

Then Eira shut her eyes and for the second time, cocooned in blood and ordure, she huddled by a clump of ivy to sleep.

* * *

Fly was limping and whining in turn. He'd slunk away from the men arguing at breakfast as to what had started the stampede, and who should go for the smith in Culworth. At least half the herd needed re-shoeing and most had lost what little condition they'd had. It wasn't until Moses Richards had shaken out his napkin and blown his nose that he realised their one dog had gone.

Too many smells, new distractions, and the brown half-breed instead of keeping straight, took the hidden turning up to

Capswell Lodge.

The dowager Lady Dunbarnie felt a draught from outside and something brush her skirts. Being of an affectionate nature she leant forwards to acquaint herself with the visitor, still keeping her considerable weight on her stick.

Fly cowered under her petticoats until he was lifted from his sanctuary and held aloft by a young man dressed more for the city than larks in the country.

"I recognise this little whipster, Mama. He's with those Taffies." Michael Macgregor's grin widened. "Time for a clean up, my friend, and none too soon at that." Still dangling the dog he went through from the kitchen to the scullery where he broke the ice on the bucket with his heel.

His mother heard the pathetic howling and covered her ears, wishing not for the first time she was deaf as well as blind, and wondering out loud why her youngest wasn't bettering himself elsewhere like William up at the locomotive works in Newcastle, or James just qualified as a physician in Edinburgh.

How the male blood thins and sours, she thought, ringing for Agnes to come and stir the fire. Maybe if Michael had come first, and maybe if Lord Dunbarnie had lived they could have stayed in Kirkcudbright and things would have been different...

"Always so many maybes, don't you agree?" To the maid who could never look at her employer's face.

"That's life, innit?"

The dowager's eyeless pinpricks stared in her direction.

"You know my one regret is that I never had a daughter. Someone to fuss over me, to take care of things..."

"So you keep saying, Ma'am."

"Tell me, Agnes," she began, settling herself at the kitchen table, "just what would you advise?"

"You mean, about *producing* one, Ma'am?" The old Dame was well past anything like that. Barren as the sow strung up in the barn. But Capswell Lodge was full of goings-on. Some too strange for words...

"Whatever."

The old retainer studied the flames then quickly tucked her sixth finger into her palm when she heard Dunbarnie's tread on the flags.

"My grandmother said to eat apples. Red ones, and four a day for the first month... " she babbled.

"Mama, this simpleton talks such utter bunkum," shouted her son from the adjoining scullery. "I don't know why we don't just send her back to her hole in the ground and hire someone whose opinion we can respect."

Agnes Larter scurried out but not before noticing his dirty boots and the wet dog, barely alive at the end of old twine as he dragged it back into the kitchen. He kissed his mother's scented cheek leaving her to fret over the possibility of sparks.

"Training," he lied, "and this Welsh runt had better learn new tricks or he'll be vittles for the hounds." He kicked its haunches for good measure as the dowager's stick quivered in anger.

"I don't know where you come from, sometimes, Michael MacGregor. Perhaps if I could summon the Devil, he'd tell me."

Her son chose not to hear. Instead let his helpmeet guide him back through the grounded clouds.

Eira woke too quickly and knew she wasn't alone.

"Fly?"

But the stranger hauled him away.

"What sort of name is that, pray? I can think of a dozen better for such a mistake."

"Who are you?"

"Just show me your pockets." The young man from Capswell Lodge squatted beside her. Beer, and the smell of carbine didn't go with the clothes, but he was more handsome than anything her side of the Aust. "You're with the Sennybridge lot aren't you?"

She paused, unsure of his tone. That name where the droves of Blacks and Shorthorns had converged now seemed so far away...

"I might be, I might not."

"A girl with spirit. Hey ho."

"I'm not a girl. I'm a young lady, and sir, you'll do me the honour of addressing me so." Her words surprised her, altering her colour. Even though she'd played Lords and Ladies countless times with her cousins Mair and Owen using stones for cups and bracken for fans, this was different.

"Well if I might enquire of your Ladyship why she's covered in manure with no silver in her hand?"

Eira fell silent with the shame of her filthy clothes, the mess of hair and even as the mist become fog she could see all too vividly the mud walls of Nant y Ffin, the midden, the feeble fire. She unbuttoned her coat and hefted it over into the next field.

"That's better." His fingers took hers. The gentleness of it brought a smile and he thought her exceptionally pretty, unlike the plate-face from Siloh. Just what his Mama had always wanted, but what a pity the old mare would never be able to see her...

They walked arm in arm, with the dog close at heel - the night demons fading as an easy ambience settled on their conversation. Past the great elm swathed in mistletoe where his shot had seen off the herd, back to his secrets and the light still guttering in the window.

Chapter 10

Wish You Were Here?

Creating settings with a difference.

Settings, both internal and external, can either drawn from your own experience or even where you've never been. From a magazine photograph or old postcard followed up by research on the internet and/or in Rough Guides books. Imagination has a massive part to play. Trust it, but back it up with interesting, perhaps little-known facts which could well affect your plot. Scottish writer Malcolm Mackay who sets his thrillers on the mean streets of Glasgow has rarely visited the city or experienced its underworld. Instead, he lives on the remote Isle of Lewis, opining how the unfamiliar attracts both writer and reader, and how as a writer, he prefers to make the imaginative leap.

Brave man! Come on over...

Like people, even the most beautiful landscape or building can hide a dark side; be deadly dangerous. Hitler planned 'The Final Solution' in one of Berlin's finest hotels in Berlin's Wannsee district, and surely those new railway lines with their commonplace cattle and horse trucks trundling east to end amongst innocuous-looking buildings, hadn't been anything more sinister?

Other buildings too, have an equally mundane appearance. Fred and Rosemary West's house in Gloucester, for example. And what could those unnamed galvanized steel barns littering the fields of Lincolnshire possibly contain? While researching *Wringland*, I found thousands of beakless broilers unable to fly. Turkeys crammed three deep on top of each other in indescribable filth. In the equally cruel practice of live animal transports, the juggernauts speeding along Europe's auto routes are now fully covered by tarpaulin. But still the giveaway slats are visible beneath these deceptive skins. Still the suffering goes on.

However, it's a fictional house, ordinary and small, on the corner of Succoth and Ash Tree Lane in the Virginia countryside, that in 2000 took the literary world by storm.

In his unique Gothic horror chiller, *House of Leaves*, Mark Z. Danielewski makes this innocuous-looking dwelling his main character. A house whose inside is bigger than the outside. Whose interior seems to change and where a distant growl can be heard from the Hallway. A house capable of killing those who stray too far.

When I speak of bravery, this work of genius has it all. Which is why I plan to mention relevant aspects of it throughout this book.

As for my own chiller thrillers and short stories, they too, begin with a setting that hits my heart. I agree with Annie Proulx, author of *The Shipping News* and *Brokeback Mountain* who's convinced that setting can often be a novel's main character - for better or worse – even shaping its human characters' psyches. If the setting's right, your characters will be in the right place.

My inspiration for *A Night With No Stars*, came after twelve long years in the Midlands, when I cajoled my husband into looking at properties for sale in mid-Wales. Little did I realize what this trip would inspire.

Our search began in October 2003 near Rhayader, a small town reminiscent of the 1950s, set in an area of Druidic ritual, with a real sense of Welsh mythology and its mysterious Sidh – or Underworld never being far away. I smelt the choking pine forests. Saw birds of prey wheeling high over flocks of sheep and their helpless lambs before pouncing. Was deafened by a massive waterfall named *Water Break its Neck* spewing foam into the sky. All these added to my growing sense of unease.

We'd arrived during the rainy season. Not ordinary rain, but steel rods coupled with a preternatural darkness even in the early afternoon. Nevertheless, we persevered and found ourselves navigating mile upon mile of a single track road until a faded estate agent's sign indicated an even more narrow track which dropped down to a pool of red mud. Almost lost in the middle of this, stood a tiny house. Victorian, yes, but a miniature version of what the agent's photographs showed.

With my husband heading back to the car in disgust, I waded through the doorless opening into that same mud decorated by bird poo and sheep droppings. Worse was the old salting slab bearing smears of fresh blood.

Scary place.

Immediately, I wondered who had once lived here and might want to again, where no-one will hear you scream. With only the wind, rain and sheep for company.

That's when my main protagonist, Lucy Mitchell pushed her way into my mind. A young, former publisher's assistant editor, determined to stay and investigate the brutal murder rumored to have taken place in that strange little house she eventually buys.

I'd already visited several publishing houses where assistant editors are daily submerged in an ever-increasing slush pile. Glamorous it is not. At literary awards and event I'd also noticed the powerful personae of many top authors, agents and publishers. A world that betrayed Lucy and her ambitions, and drove her westwards.

Many people cling to dreams of a better life despite what reality might be telling them. Lucy is no different, and *A Night With No Stars* shows how her dream is gradually dismantled amidst severe sibling rivalry and a climate of lies. Where brutal ancient myths and legends play as much a part as the inhabitants and landscape of rural Powys.

I began writing this chiller in long-hand straight after we returned home, using a chunky, supermarket re-fill pad, and finished the first draft after a year, before serious editing on my computer. I was fortunate to have David Shelley as my publisher at Allison & Busby, who allowed me a completely free reign with my theme and characters.

As for *Malediction*, it's set in those parts of France I've actually visited. From the capital's familiar tourist traps to grim suburbs such as Drancy, home to the largest number of Jewish deportations during the last war. From the economically deprived northeast to the wind-blasted vineyards of the Corbières in the south. All photographed, together with my own detailed sketches for future reference.

You never know when records like these might come in useful. I also spent time inside the awesome splendor of Notre Dame Cathedral, listening to Pérotin's sublime organ music. He's my ruthless, duplicitous protagonist Robert Vidal's favorite composer. More churches followed, this time in the Ardennes region, where steep hills topped by simpler houses of worship suddenly erupted from the flat farmland. Here, carvings which at first glance seemed attractive, proved to be anything but. The word 'carnage' still comes to mind. I also discovered what appeared to be a highly secretive monastery near Vézelay, replete with blood-soaked marble crucifixions. Back home, still fascinated by what I'd seen, I discovered, while reading *The Holy Blood and The Holy Grail*, this was the headquarters of the Prieuré de Sion. Another fascinating subject.

Further travels took me to a small, depressed town in the industrialized Vosges. The scene of a mysterious crime in 1984 in which four year-old Grégory Vilemin had been found drowned a grimy canal with both hands tied together and his balaclava pulled down over his eyes. This cruel crime has fixated France ever since, because it revealed the presence of 'Le Corbeau' – a poison pen writer whose work had harassed Grégory's family since 1981 and destroyed more than one life. It inspired my published short story *Sword Lilies* where a secret and vindictive letter writer wreaks havoc in her village. *Bloodstream* has an even more controversial theme than *Malediction*. The race to produce a legitimate, Bourbon heir to the French throne.

So, I hope these accounts give you glimpses of how places and events associated with them, can haunt the writer long after the physical journey is over.

Country villages still seem to have plenty of mileage as settings, including for two current, prime-time BBC thrillers, *Mayday* and *Broadchurch*. Both with familiar themes of missing children. Clearly, the rural idyll still rules, but try and make yours somehow different.

In a Cumberland village, an ancient curse prevented the Council from moving a huge and dangerous mesolithic stone, while a small Cornish community still celebrates its ancient and slightly ominous 'Darkie Day' every year. The list is endless. Take a look!

Other popular settings include Wartime Berlin/Eastern Europe, South Africa, Australia, certain parts of the USA (NY/LA/Chicago), France (Provence and Paris), Scotland (Glasgow, Edinburgh and the Shetland Isles) and Ireland (Dublin). All this apart from the wave of Nordic Noir hitting our shores.

Brighton is home to Peter Guttridge's excellent thrillers, *City of Dreadful /Night*, *The Last King of Brighton* and *The Thing Itself*. *The Devil's Moon*, fourth in his series, continues to delve into what the town's tourists shouldn't see.

London still looms large, and Hanna Jameson's *Something You Are* is the first in her London Underground series, which features a hitman with a heart. If this city is your choice too, finding a more unusual aspect of it could still pay off. Spitalfields, like so many upmarket areas, has a fascinating history.

Vienna too, is a hardy perennial, and in Jed Rubenfield's elegant thriller, *The Death Instinct*, he not only takes us to Sigmund Freud's home there, but also to Paris, Prague and Washington DC after a massive bomb attack on New York's Wall

Street in September 1920. Hawaii is the setting for *The Tsunami Countdown*, by Boyd Morrison.

Michael Ridpath however, is setting his latest successful series of thrillers in Iceland, while Kevin Sampson's *The Killing Pool* is inspired by the port of Liverpool, where lawlessness is literally on the edge of the Irish Sea.

Do your own research on Amazon books, in bookshops and libraries to identify 'hotspots' to avoid. For me, Egypt's barren White Desert - one of the most bizarre and haunting places on this planet – has it all. And is so far, virgin territory.

USA thriller writer, C.J. Box uses Rocky Mountain West for his Game Warden Joe Pickett to patrol, which makes a refreshing change from well-trodden urban scenes. His latest, *Force of Nature* draws heavily on this atmospheric environment, however, Adrian Magson, creator of the Inspector Lucas Rocco series set in 1963 rural Picardie, and the high-octane ex-MI5 Harry Tate thrillers, wisely cautions us with...

'One of the problems with writing thrillers... is the more detail about the setting and circumstance that you put in, the more likely it is that you will lose some of the pace of the story.' Good points.

Exercises

i) Choose 4 possible settings either that you've visited or imagined, that will stand out for their originality. For each one, add the following – in reality or fictionally...

ii) How have they changed over the years?

iii) What significant events have happened there?

iv) What might happen there?

v) What literally lies beneath? Research the geology. I.e; parts of the UK are built on disused mines. On grave-yards. (Our brand new house was, and it was haunted!) Some are situated on fault lines at risk of earthquakes.

vi) What myths and legends are/might be associated with

them? Remember, the past doesn't always lie very deep beneath the 'civilizing' veneer of Tarmac...

vii) In at least 200 words, describe each chosen setting or select a part of it which may be significant to you later on. Paint as vivid a picture of each as you can, invoking the particular season, the temperature, light quality or lack of it, smells, and sounds.

Interestingly, in a writing workshop given by the late Julian Rathbone at the Winchester Writers' Conference, his description of a market in Marrakech solely from his imagination was judged to be much more real than that from an actual visit! And how about the 2006 Costa Book Award winner Stef Penny, whose *'The Tenderness of Wolves'* set in Canada was written without her ever having set foot there? Bravery certainly paid off for her!

viii) Buy, beg or borrow *House of Leaves* by Mark Z. Danielewski.

Examples

a) Johan Theorin's *The Darkest Room* gives an unforgettable account of how the manor house at Eel Point on the Island of Oland was built from pieces of shipwrecked wood. The author was brought up here, and its bleak mood seeps through every page.

b) Frankie Holt in my published thriller *Come and be Killed*, was adopted by the Holts as a newborn baby, and bears grudges not only against her step-family, but the mother who abandoned her. With her own creepy, 'newborn' doll, Ellie, she moves to Malvern - a town almost suffocated by its surrounding hills - to begin her killing.

Christ, the woman was heavy. More than heavy. Nothing at Briarfield had prepared her for this. For a start, it was all going to be uphill. Frankie cursed as she prised both bare legs out of the boot and began dragging the body to the closest clump of high ferns in a hollow below the summit of North Hill. Then something caught her eye. A blue and white police cordon surrounded the spot where that bonfire had been; where she'd met Carol Piper. Just to see it quickened her movements. Made her forget to breathe. She should have realized this wasn't the best place to hide something so substantial, and yet...

It was as if her mistake with the stick was adding to her punishment. If only she'd listened to Mrs Beavis and kept control of herself. And then it occurred to her that if and when the aged ballerina was ever found, it would look as if the man due to inherit her estate, and already under suspicion for an immigrant's disappearance, was taunting the pigs with another crime. Pushing his luck.

"Yessss..."

By now, the corpse was already attracting more flies.

Frankie scoured the wild grazed hilltops stretching away for as far as the eye could see and, apart from the moving speck of a distant dog walker, there wasn't another soul around. She must get back to Teme House straight away. Burn the walking stick to make it look like her client had wandered off, and then carry on as normal.

Finally, she must clear her head. Get her mind sorted and not forget why she was really here.

Using her handy latex gloves, she crammed Merle's tiara back on her head and those dentures back into her mouth. Then she pulled her white knickers down to her knees. She slithered back to the Fiesta, relieved to notice that its tire tracks were merged amongst many and her footprints blurred with those who'd come up for the bonfires last Friday. However, her satisfaction was short-lived. Ellie looked too passive. Too detached from every-thing that she, her caring mother had just gone through.

"You could have stopped me fucking killing her," she

snapped. "But you just lay there. I mean, if you'd made a noise, or said something, I'd still have a nice roof over my head. You as well."

She reversed into a muddy lay by and rejoined the track leading from the road.

"You just bloody lay there, Ellie. You let me hit her all those times. You *must* have heard what she was yelling at me. Now look..." She nudged her, then noticed a posse of mountain bikers approaching around an oncoming bend. She slowed up, lowering her shaded eyes as they passed, missing their waves of acknowledgement, scared they might stop on the incline for a chat and get a good look at her. Be unwanted witnesses...

Frankie passed The Gables yet again and saw Brownlow's Jeep had gone. She also swore she could see a thin tense face at the lower bay window on the left.

She stepped on the gas, not caring now that Ellie had tipped out of her seat and was lying on the floor with both her legs in the air.

"You stop there till you've said sorry an' all," she muttered. "You're the reason we'll be poor all over again. D'you know that?"

Those black clouds which had congregated over the top of North Hill seemed to be multiplying, obliterating the last small scraps of blue, so that by the time she turned in through Teme House's double gates, letting out a gasp of relief that the Production Manager's 4X4 wasn't there either, a sly rain had begun to fall.

c) From Suzanne Ruthven's atmospheric and original thriller, *Whittlewood*. What's excellent about this is short piece where Alex Martin arrives at Charlotte Manning's house, is how the author takes us from the general to the particular. From an overview to those vivid, scarlet leaves...

Hunter's Moon was the last house in the village - a beautifully preserved Elizabethan farmhouse, which, like its neighbours, had remained completely unspoiled by tasteless modernisation. The mellow stonework gleamed in the fading sunlight as a light autumn breeze pulled the last scarlet leaves from an ancient Virginia creeper. As the house was situated on a sharp bend in the road, Alex swung the Austin Healey under the stone archway into an immaculate cobbled stable yard, rather than risk leaving it outside to the mercy of any passing local vandals.

In the shadows under the archway he noticed a door and instead of walking around to the front of the house, he announced his presence loudly with the iron knocker. A light showed through the fanlight and above the glass he could see a carved wooden mask, coloured red and white - a Japanese charm to prevent evil spirits from entering the house.

The door was opened by a short, plump woman with bright robin eyes and greying hair that still showed evidence of an unsuccessful home perm. Almost totally enveloped by a large floral, wrap-over pinafore, she was engaged in removing flour from her hands with a tea towel. Half relieved and half disappointed at this seemingly normal apparition, Alexander Martin gave his name.

d) Study chapter 6 from my chiller, *A Night With No Stars*, where Lucy Mitchell nears Wern Goch, the house she's hoping to buy. Try and edit it further to improve its effectiveness. Consider: i) words used as padding, ii) overwriting, iii) could the pace be improved? iv) Were you there on her shoulder? v) Did Mark's POV before the end, add to the story?

6.

I have fled as a wolf cub, I have fled as a wolf in the wilderness...
    Taliesin

The now deeply rutted track abruptly turned downhill - its gradient as vertiginous as a Big Dipper run, except that this particular route was awash with surplus water and large loose stones which lifted her wheels, made the car lurch perilously from side to side, and sent her book flying to the floor.

At last Lucy reached the bottom which was under at least a foot of mud and saw a further track lead off on the right. At its corner stood a washed-out sign saying RAVENSTONE.

Thank God.

And, without realising, she began to breathe normally again.

But her relief was short-lived. She peered through the filthy windscreen and noticed with dismay a high ridge of grass between the ruts. Almost too high, she thought, slipping into first gear, just in case. The Rav stalled, again and again, trapped on this unkempt island until with a surge of power, she pressed onwards as the track opened out on to a weed-strewn hardcore driveway.

She stared in amazement at what lay at the end of it. Was this huge Gothic pile real or was she hallucinating? Anything was possible after what she'd just endured. She blinked, switched the smeary wipers to top speed for a better view, without success, and the longer she stared at the building's forbidding bleakness, so did thoughts of Transylvania stay stubbornly in her mind.

While the visitor waited, the rain strengthened and drove down mercilessly on both man, beast and the boggy land they shared while the forestry worker made his way round to the blind western side of the Hall. Mark knelt down next to the unmarked spot where his mother now lay and used his bare hands to gouge out a small hollow alongside her. Just as he was smoothing the top layer of soil over the pink silk bundle, he heard an unfamiliar car's engine close by.

He sat back on his haunches and stared in the direction of the access track beyond the drive, convinced that neither Bryn

Evans's Defender nor Dai Fish's Transit was paying a call. For a start, there was some hesitation going on with the engine idling then revving. His pulse quickened; the carotid pumped in his neck. Maybe Miss Mitchell had arrived and was changing her mind after all. And why not? He'd worked hard enough to prevent her getting there, but, if she still insisted on viewing his den, at least that blood on the salting slab would be sure to put her off. No way was he going to clean up and sanitise the place as he'd been instructed. Those souvenirs were all he had.

His wait was soon rewarded, for a muddy metallic blue poser's car appeared at the end of the track and struggled up the last few yards to the turning area in front of the Hall. After a few moments he saw the slim figure of a young woman wearing jeans and a white t-shirt under a denim jacket emerge from the driver's side door and, having checked the car's bodywork on both sides, began making her way towards the Hall. He saw several sheets of printed matter in her hand and with a lurch of his heart recognised the estate agency's distinctive logo on the top page. So, here she was. At last.

Chapter 11

Research Needn't Be A Chore

It's your metal detector!

Once you have decided upon your setting/s, the real fun starts. If you've chosen somewhere real on the map, and it's within travelling distance, then go. I'd never have found out or imagined what lurked around the mouth of the River Nene unless I'd been there many times for *Wringland*. The area felt so haunted, and local people I met confirmed it. Such places that inspire fear and excitement in the author, will also stir the reader.

Discover the history, the economics, the geology, the dialect of your chosen setting/s. Talk to local people and relevant experts. I've always found them extremely helpful, and when your book is published, an acknowledgement of this help is always appreciated.

If your main setting is fictionalized, you still need to 'explore' it, perhaps by locating somewhere similar.

When I'd settled in Northampton, and began researching my second chiller, *Cloven* in its helpful Records Office, the then Mayor had no idea that his town centre and many villages to the south of the county had, before 1832 and the arrival of trains, witnessed scenes more akin to the Wild West. Hordes of Welsh Black cattle had surged along the narrow country lanes and, according to local accounts, 'nursemaids rushed outside to fetch the children to safety.' A telling detail of how the Welsh drovers' thirsty cattle 'licked at the puddles as they went' has stayed with me ever since.

The more I read, the more everything from that era came alive, and I was back in time, amidst this turmoil. The same that Siân Richards, my plucky, disabled fourteen year-old protagonist also witnesses. During lunchtimes between my Adult Education teaching, I'd sit in one of these village pubs and talk to whoever I could. What they readily revealed was serious criminality going on behind some of the pretty ironstone cottages' doors and smart looking farmsteads, and how the local police often seemed powerless.

All this, I used, and more, including the Assize Records for the then Northampton Gaol which opened up an even bleaker world of young lives ending with 'the drop.' Of convicted murderers' last words and their often ignominious last resting places. Of crimes which today would merit less than five years behind bars. All this furnished my work, and you too can be rewarded.

Place names can be tricky. Phil Rickman, author of the wonderfully spooky Merrily Watkins series set in Herefordshire, never uses real names for his villages, but Hereford stays the same. In *Cold Remains*, I kept the name of Rhandirmwyn, the Carmarthenshire village because its disused lead mine was a significant feature. No complaints yet, touch wood, despite some seriously dark, fictional events happening there.

Your research may involve drugs, firearms, chemicals, bomb-making equipment, aeronautics, the police, prisons, law courts etc. and for this you'll need material too diverse to be added to my list of useful reference books and magazines. The internet will be incredibly useful, but take care with copyrighted material. Paraphrase and rewrite to avoid problems, and if you know of anyone expert in your required field, they may be willing to advise you. If later on, once you have a publisher's contract, you can join the Crime Writers' Association, where there are many members with the above specialties who offer their services to fellow members.

Exercises

i) Names often reflect the area. E.g., in Lincolnshire, many end in 'toft.' What are yours?

ii)   What are your other interesting 'finds?'

iii) How do you envisage these affecting the plot?

iv) What research still needs to be done?

v)   Who might you need to approach?

Examples

a) From *Cloven*, where Ivan Browning in the library, learns more about the Northampton Assizes.

Ivan folded the paper and stuffed it in his pocket. Either way, the poor sod had been a victim. He got up to look around.

The shelf labeled 'Northamptonshire Life and Times' contained a self-published work on the Lamport steam railway, two thin volumes on the growth of the canal system, and a thickish brown book with worn corners: *Notorious Gangs in Northamptonshire* by Mervyn Stanton, published in 1907.

Ivan's heart began racing. He cursed inwardly at having to share a table, but there was no alternative. However, the old guy opposite him had gone to sleep. While Ivan thumbed through the pages which contained Stanton's own versions of trial accounts as well as bleak engravings of the accused, the sky outside growled with thunder and the heavens opened.

By midday, he'd become acquainted with Thomas the Baker who'd turned 'approver' to save his skin, with Bacaunt and his tribe, with John de Aston and the Culworth Gang whose villainous days ended on Northampton Racecourse in August 1787. Next, after the Hollowfield Four, came George Catherall, 'Captain Slash', who was hanged shoeless on the New Drop in 1826. Finally something which made Ivan snatch his breath. It was a heading at the foot of one page: 'Northampton Lent Assizes of 28 March 1830', followed by the names *Luke, Noah and Arthur DAWSON*. The following pages had been crudely torn out.

He checked again carefully – there was nothing more to be had on them, and the proof was three jagged page edges close to the stitching of the spine.

His scraping chair startled the old man from his slumbers.

Ivan headed over to the issue desk and showed the damage to a girl who, judging by her youth, was probably there on Work Experience. She was busy stacking returned books onto a wooden trolley. 'Have you seen this vandalism?' He slapped Stanton's work down in front of her.

'Oh Lord.' A heavily ringed finger trailed along the tear. 'I'd better show this to Mr Gifford.'

Mr Gifford, too, fingered the rough edges where the yellowed pages had once been. 'Why would anyone want to do a thing like that? I don't think we can find another copy of this either. It's out of print.' He checked the details on the fragile flyleaf. 'Wilton and May stopped publishing just before the last war. I'm terribly sorry.'

'Did anyone take over their business? I mean, another publisher maybe? It *is* important.'

The older man frowned. 'No. They went bankrupt.

What was it you were interested in?' he asked, skimming the volume.

'The Dawsons, tried in March 1830… Luke, Noah and Arthur.'

'Ah,' said the librarian enigmatically. 'Well there's the County Record Office, of course. Or, if you want to save petrol, you could get in touch with my brother.'

'Your brother?'

'Yes, he's called Charlie Gifford, and he covered quite a few local criminals in his dissertation at the University College last summer. It was also about enclosures and the growth of non-conformism, something like that. He's a mature student, working for his MA now. I can give you his number, if you like, as he lives only round the corner from the Leisure Centre.' He scribbled a phone number on a scrap of paper and handed it to Ivan. Then, picking up the damaged book, he marked it with a big black cross. 'Mmm. Someone didn't want that section left too public.'

'And I'll give you one guess who that was,' Ivan muttered to himself, charging through the sleeting rain to a public phone box opposite.

A boyish voice responded on the student historian's answerphone. Ivan left his message, and then went in search of lunch. A ham and mustard bap with a liberal spread of melted cheese on the top. Something filling and calorific for the afternoon ahead, at St Thomas's church.

Chapter 12

Weather

Beef it up!

Getting this right can make a profound difference to your chiller thriller. The weather can also, like your setting/s become a main character. Another obstacle to your hero/heroine's/others' goals. Extremes can add a sub-plot or two. Can change people's behavior. You have a big opportunity here when describing the weather to your reader, to avoid the tired old clichés. I.e; the rain *trickled* down his back. Snowflakes *fluttered* to the ground. Dip into that Thesaurus again!

Exercises

i) Think back to whenever you were exposed to extreme conditions. Where? What did it feel like? Smell like? Yes, flood water can smell. Spare no detail!

ii) Write down what item of extreme weather news - past or present, or of an invented future - has stayed in your mind? Why?

iii) Because of the imagery?

iv) The effect it had on human/animal/insect life?

v) Because you believe it was triggered by human/other behavior?

vi) Write at least 200 words describing what would be your worst possible weather scenario. Beef up the visceral sensations. Take us with you!

Examples

a) From chapter 2 of *Carcass*, my second thriller in the ex-DI John Lyon trilogy. Here, in west Wales, seventeen year-old Laure Deschamps is exercising her favorite racehorse.

2.

Remember the First Circle...you deserve nothing and God will see to it you get nothing but ice and snow and the deaths of your children and everyone fooled into loving you...

Friday 11th March 2.15pm.

Christ, it was cold enough to freeze your bollocks off, I thought. Or your tits. Whatever. I was used to this kind of temperature in the Poitou, but the Welsh variety came spiked with ice and a west wind so fierce, my face beneath my riding hat, had frozen into a grimace.

As for my mount, Vervain, the 5/4 on favorite to land tomorrow's Sprucewood Novices Chase at Chepstow, he'd leapt out of our training gallops like a two year-old, almost unseating me as he'd landed, and now look...

He'd spotted the sea below the distant cliff edge, and was fighting me, his double bit and an extra tight surcingle to get there.

Merde...

He was out of control. His head stuck forwards with the restraining bit already dangling uselessly from the side of his mouth. I saw that black sea getting closer with every stride. If I messed up this last and most important work-out, I'd be relegated to stable chores. Or worse, given a one-way rail ticket to Cardiff to make my own way in life. Why? Because Papa, Alain Deschamps, racehorse trainer *extraordinaire,* allowed not one make-weight in his successful yard. Even if I *was* his only daughter.

"Whoa!" I screamed.

Fat chance.

Vervain was 'away with the fairies,' as they say over here. Chasing the looping seagulls. Chasing the wind so fast I couldn't breathe. Couldn't hold on, and the white-turreted Sea Breeze Hotel with its windows of happy diners, was the last thing I registered before hitting the ground and passing out.

b) The first part of chapter 2 from *The Leper House* – the third in my ex-DI John Lyon trilogy, where the exceptional heat is making forty-two year-old Stanley Bulling of Wombwell Farm in Norfolk even more resentful.

2.

Thursday 15th July 1920 midday.

Everything's so bloody hot. Even the pitchfork's iron handle Pa's given me to use to clean out the pig pens. And why me? I keep asking mesen? Why not that good-for-nothing Johnny Foreigner still snoring away in the barn? To be honest, I've half a mind to jab both prongs into his black belly and hear him squeal, just like our hogs at the Michaelmas killing.

Sweat were runnin' into me eyes and the pig shit stink blocked my nose, so I tied my neckerchief around my face and set to. Separating straw from the rest. Feeling me guts rise up in revolt.

"Don't leave 'em too long in the yard," Pa had instructed from the comfort of his armchair in the farmhouse. "Or they'll burn. And then where'd we be?"

I'd not replied. Never did. What were the point? He'd beat me down every time, like he did with Ma. Me the slave. The fucking workhorse of Wombwell Farm. Sometimes I wished I'd joined up with the Norfolk Regiment like most of them others round here, and been one of the glorious fallen. Yes, glorious, because what the fuck was glorious about what I was doing now?

Forty wasted years…

The army'd said I had a job to do here for king and country. Feeding all the ungrateful spongers, more like. But that weren't the real reason, was it? Only me and the birds know what that was. And they've probably all been shot by now.

Enough.

I gripped the pitchfork lower down its shaft and, holding it up like a lance, made for the hay barn. Even though the sun beat down on its old tin roof, inside was as black as night. Two crows left the main beam and brushed past me as I stood in the entrance beating out those flies still trapped in me hair.

I thought again of Ma and Pa with their wrinkly, white feet up, waitin' for the money to roll in. Money *I* were makin' for them, and yet they'd still not made a will. Or so they'd said. *If* all this was coming to me, I thought, searching again for the stowaway from Mauritius who'd crawled to our door a month ago, I'd sell it quicker than you could take a squat. I'd move down to London. See some life. Be anonymous. Even find mesen a nice piece o' meat because no-one here had ever looked at me in that way, which is why, last spring I'd let that dumb Susan Deakins kid from Doric Farm have it front and back three times and once more for luck.

But I'd not worked things out, 'ad I? What if she'd done drawings, used sign language to get her revenge on me? Well, all I could say to that was she wouldn't any more. But I've still kept her liberty bodice button that fell off at the time. Surely I were allowed *one* little souvenir?

c) Do read *The Murdered House* by Pierre Magnan. (In translation) The wild weather in Provence in both 1896 and post 1919 is another main character. The author immerses his readers in its ruthless power. You won't be disappointed.

Chapter 13

Who Goes There?

It's time to give birth to your main protagonists.

Names are crucial. First, middle and surnames can reflect a particular place, even a continent or an era. The first name is usually at the whim of the parent or other. In Wales, many people are known by their middle names, and the trend for women to hyphenate their maiden names with their partners' surnames is increasing. So being double-barrelled doesn't necessarily equate with 'posh.'

Names can be a blessing or a burden. Vincent van Gogh was given the first name of his recently dead sibling. That's some start in life. And what if your perfectly decent main protagonist is called Rudy Himmler?

Some British surnames have almost become obsolete. E.g., Clegg, Chips, Harred, Hatman, Rummage, while Jarsdel, Nithercott, Raynott and Woodbead already are. If your material is historical, check out names from your chosen era/s, whereas a futuristic chiller thriller gives you more leeway.

In his superb, original thriller, *Eye Contact* by Fergus MacNeill, we learn on page 1 that his creepy, murdering perfectionist is called Robert Naysmith. After this, he's either Rob to his girlfriend or simply Naysmith as we witness with mounting horror, his sociopathic progress.

Maybe there *is* no name for the unwanted fetus who, in some parts of Ireland, was doomed to spend an afterlife in limbo. No name either, or several false ones if your living character with dissociative anonymity operates in the murky world of the internet...

Go for a variation in ages too. As for what your characters look like, you may well use a dream or a memory or come across a photograph or painting which comes close to what you want. Karin Fossum, another fine Nordic *noir* writer, even claims to 'see' her characters lined up outside her cottage door 'waiting for me to deal with them.'

I write my chiller thrillers' first drafts in longhand so that I can also draw my characters on the opposite page.

I hear many stories from fellow published authors who claim that some of their characters simply announce themselves at odd moments, when least expected. Whatever your method, they must be memorable to the reader. Tom Ripley in Patricia Highsmith's *The Talented Mr. Ripley*, is a unique creation. A snake in the grass if ever there was, whose boyish looks disguise a seething jealousy and unrequited homosexual love for the doomed playboy, Dickie Greenleaf.

As I outlined in my introduction on page 5, creating characters is all rather a mysterious process. Some would say almost psychic. Actors 'becoming' their characters, too, comes close, and do we believe Daniel Day-Lewis who claims to have 'seen' his late father whilst being on stage.

Exercise

i) Who are your main protagonists? Give middle names too, if significant.

ii) When were they born?

iii) Their ages when you meet them?

iv) What's their enduring childhood memory? (Remember, a false memory or retrospective construct is not uncommon.)

v) Their dreams and desires?

vi) Being trusting is said to be the key to happiness. Are they?

vii) What's the worst they can do?

viii) And the best?

ix) As in *Suspect* by Robert Crais, don't rule out an animal or two.

x) Keep thinking about these characters. They'll become as real to you as anyone else.

Remember, you the author, have to be in their heads. The reader, on their shoulders.

Remember too, your reader expects an emotional experience from the moment the book or e-book version they've chosen is in their hands. So whoever carries your story is crucial, and you *can* play God. Unlike author Lionel Shriver who, replying to the question why she'd not had any children, used the startling analogy of opening the back door and not knowing who's coming in.

Example

In *Malediction*, The duplicitous but handsome Robert Vidal and reluctant recruit Dominique Mathieu visit a flat in Drancy, Paris, where Colette's son is being held prisoner. Vidal has helped put him there. Mathieu rebels...

"Nice place." Vidal disengaged himself while Mathieu hung back, taking in the dirt, the neglect on what was a typical example of post-war urban architecture. It had a secret and forbidding air. Even the list of occupants individually encased behind Plexiglas were almost bleached out, and Vidal's finger trailed from top to bottom without much fervour.

"Where's Plagnol's name?" Mathieu asked.

"Idiot. It's Lautin. Charles Lautin. Very clever, I must say." Then Vidal stopped, took a step back. "I can't."

"What d'you mean, can't? We've *got* to see if Bertrand's alright."

Vidal scanned the building and shivered. It was as silent as a house of the Dead, and for the first time, he looked Mathieu squarely in the eye.

"C'mon. Let's get back."

"No. I'm going in."

Vidal restrained him and Mathieu felt his panic as if it was his own. He took the advantage and pressed the buzzer faintly marked C L. No sound, nothing, and no intercom either. "Shit."

"You're on your own."

"I'm not, damn you."

"What you saying then?"

"Haven't you heard of God?" And as though fortified, Mathieu pressed another with SUZELLE Mme, in pale italics.

Vidal struck him across the mouth. Warm blood cradled his tongue so that when the elderly occupant of flat 7 called from above, he was unable to reply.

"Who's there?" she cried. "I'll call the police."

"That's what we want," Mathieu managed to burble.

"Shut up you!" Vidal hit him again. "It's er... just a little disagreement Madame. Sorry to disturb you... "

"There's someone in 15 who could be dying!" The Breton yelled, free for a split second. "It's urgent!"

"You imbecile." Vidal had him by the hair and crushed him against the wall with a silent strength. "We came, we cannot see because there is after all, nothing to see, and we leave because I do not wish to be maggot fodder just yet. OK?"

Suddenly the sound of keys and a cobwebbed light over the door giving them no quarter.

"Don't move." Vidal, the music-lover tried an embrace, but Mathieu was ready, pushing the old woman to one side and taking the stairs behind her three at a time. "Come back you bloody fool!" Boomed up the stairwell behind him, as on the fourth floor he found 15a on a scruffy red door, and heard a low moaning in the brief stillness before Vidal reached him. Mathieu's fists pummelled the wood. He shrieked to Bertrand that his maman and Jesus still loved him and not to lose his faith, before Vidal felled him against the banisters.

A door opposite opened briefly then closed and Madame Suzelle's screams diminished as she too found sanctuary.

Vidal's watch was fast and in frustration he slapped Mathieu some more before wiping away the worst of the mess. He pressed his ear tight to the paintwork. The Bébé was calling for his mother, calling and choking, and a trickle of something invaded the landing, reaching his boot. His own lips moved on a whisper, not a prayer, then he dragged Mathieu down past the bedridden and the drunks, down towards the sound of the midnight bell from Notre Dame de la Consolation.

Chapter 14

Looks To Die For?

In Victorian times, having the wrong physiognomy could land you in trouble. Too big a forehead, a jutting, anthropoid jaw, and you could be locked away. We still have ingrained perceptions of beauty and ugliness, and too often are repelled by one and seduced by the other. A lovely young woman is far less likely to arouse suspicion than her opposite, yet Hitchcock deployed innocent-looking guilties and guilty-looking innocents until they in turn, almost become a cliché.

First impressions count, although they may be inaccurate. To filter the most memorable description/s of your main characters for the reader, you need to have plenty of information under your belt. Meanwhile, watch those around you. The variation in eyebrows and ear lobes is extraordinary.

UK Passports used to ask for 'any distinguishing features. What do your main characters possess? Oscar Pistorious, the South African Paralympics runner recently arrested for murder, has a stirring and lengthy quote from the first book of Corinthians tattooed on his left shoulder.

Exercises

i) Write a detailed physical description of your 4 main characters. Leave no stone unturned. Even down to toenails! Skin texture is useful. The Japanese think British people smell of dairy produce, while others say 'you can always tell another's character by their shoes.'

ii) This is an odd question, but interesting. How do your characters' heads sit on their shoulders?

iii) If able-bodied, how do they walk/run?

iv) Let *them* describe themselves.

   v) Let another character describe one of them. This can be interesting and tell us something more about the viewer.

Examples

a) In *Cold Remains*, Helen Jenkins first meets Jason Robbins.

Once in Swansea, near the station, Helen parked her Ignis up on the kerb outside a greasy spoon cafe and switched off its grunting wipers. Her curiosity about the emergency arrival now outweighed her resentment at his nerve. Perhaps he was as old as Mr Flynn. Or older. Perhaps he had a shady past best kept hidden. Even a wife and kids somewhere. As she manually locked her car, and tried opening her knackered umbrella against the wind, she realized with a churning pulse, she was soon about to find out.

Commuters. Swarms of them, striding, clack-clacking along the platform towards her like a dark, rough sea. Who was she looking for? There'd been no description asked for or given, during that early morning phone call. Just that Jason Robbins would be wearing a black leather jacket plus jeans, and carrying a battered suitcase.

And then she spotted it. Attached to a guy in yes, black leather and stone-washed denim who seemed paler than his travelling companions, with a more wary look in his eye. His gelled brown hair bristled from his head, and from the lobe of his left ear, glistened a small stud.

Not her sort at all.

However, she'd been trained to observe, to look hard at her subject, and saw that although that suitcase with its rusted steel corners, seemed mediaeval, the shoes weren't cheap. Nor the jacket that hung from a pair of broad shoulders. As he handed his ticket to the waiting inspector, she noticed there was no wedding ring. She also wondered what job he did to be able to take an extra week off. Why so important to come to Wales now, and whether or not he had a return ticket tucked away somewhere.

He glanced up, caught her eye, then walked past her, probably thinking that a representative of the grandly-named Heron House would at least look the part.

"Hi." She ran after him, pushing her wet hair off her face. Aware how naff she looked in the black suit not worn since her uncle's funeral three years ago. "Are you by any chance Jason Robbins?"

He stopped, turned to face her, that same wary expression giving way to a smile. "Are you Patsy Palmer?"

"Funny, not. I'm Helen Jenkins from Heron House." She held out her right hand like Mr Flynn had told her to do. "Welcome to wet and windy Wales. Or, as they say here, Croeso i Gymru."

Note; the now fatherless Helen's no siren, but since leaving art college has been missing the company of young men her age. I wanted to give the reader the impression that perhaps the door might be opening to a relationship with this not terribly promising wannabe writer.

b) In my short chiller, *Tea for Two,* ex-con Carl Dwyer, now in his late sixties is being interviewed about a cold case crime from his youth. The cop has just shown him a black and white photograph taken near Tower Bridge and asked him to point himself out.

"There I am, in the distance, walking away from them others." I say, pointing at the skinniest kid with the whitest legs. "See? D'you need a magnifying glass?"

"No, Mr Dwyer. Just some answers. Why were you walking away?"

"Fed up of being called Fatso, Big Ears and the rest. I remember thinking I'd better things to do than hang around taking shit like that."

"Just you?"

"Yes."

"Think again."

"I don't get it," I say. "You had a tip-off?"

"What about?"

This is a trick...

"Nothing."

I was brought here hot and sweaty, but not any more. Quite the opposite. I'm looking for my gloves to warm up my fingers, but they've gone missing.

"How about the evening of September 10th 1950?" He goes on, and I can't help sneaking a look at his shaved neck. His clean, shiny skin.

Like I've said, I've never trusted the Fuzz. Why should I, given my history? But this one, young enough to be my own son, seems kosher enough. Even the brew he's brought in for me is drinkable. Although his smile is meant to crack my memory that's hardened like cement, you try recalling stuff that happened that long ago. It's no joke, 'specially since there's been so much water under the bridge - Tower Bridge, to be precise.

Note; I deliberately chose to use Carl's POV and the present tense to create a sense of immediacy, and I hope his brief observation of the cop is enough at this stage. The reader of both short story collections where this is published, will know his suit is too tight, and later, that his teeth are noticeably large and perfectly formed.

Chapter 15

Your Chosen Few's Nearest But Not Necessarily Dearest

Are they a best friend? A close colleague? A family foe in sheep's clothing? A pavement angel, fireside Devil whose dichotomous personality can cause untold harm?

Exercises

i) Draw a circle in the middle of a blank page, and add your main character's name. Link other circles to this, containing other names. Closer circles will denote a closer relationship. These can extend back a long way. E.g., if your main character is an elderly man, then a childhood friend could be added. Even an imaginary one...

ii) Do any of these characters hold positions of trust? (Not only as parents or other relations or guardians etc) E.g., doctor/nurse/teacher/priest/funeral director/financial adviser etc.

iii) What is the worst they can do?

iv) And the best?

Examples

a) In this chapter of Sarah Rayne's *Spider Light*, we meet someone whose respectable exterior hides a dark and complex heart. Whose later actions also affect the present.

Chapter Four

Thomasina Forrester did not much care for music. A lot of time-wasting and flummery. But the thing was that Maud liked music, in fact music played quite a big part in Maud's life – piano lessons and practice, to say nothing of unutterably tedious musical evenings at Maud's house when guests had perforce to listen to recitals and solos – and so it looked as if music would have to play a big part in Thomasina's life as well. But she would accept that and cope with it. She would accept and cope with anything if it meant getting Maud in her bed.

It was remarkable that after all these years of love'em and leave'em Thomasina should find herself bowled over, knocked for a loop, by a pretty face, and a sweet smile, but so it was. Maud Lincoln. Utter perfection. Quantities of fair, fluffy hair, and a china-doll complexion and a bedpost waist. And just seventeen. A delightful age for a girl, seventeen. Fresh, unspoiled. *Ripe...* The smile that very few people saw curved Thomasina's lips as she considered Maud Lincoln's unspoiled freshness. Rather a pity about the name, however. Gardens and black-bat nights, and a green sound to the surname. With a face like that she should be called something more lyrical. Imogen or Daphnis or Heloise. Still, what was in a name? And once the bedroom lights were out and you were in bed together with your clothes off, who cared? More importantly, how should she go about this latest seduction?

Gentlemen, when engaged in the pursuit of a lady, often plied the object of their desire with wine, in fact Thomasina's second cousin Simon had once told her that there was nothing like a judicious drop of wine to get rid of inhibitions. Thomasina had merely smiled and had not commented, but she had thought to herself: aha, I must remember that one, and had indeed remembered it, and to very good purpose on more than one occasion.

But Maud Lincoln was not one who could be coaxed and tricked into bed by the use of alcohol. Maud would have to be seduced very gradually, almost without her realising what was happening. That could mean a vastly frustrating few weeks for Thomasina, but if it went on for too long she could always make one of her discreet trips to London; there was that cat-faced child in Seven Dials, all of fifteen years old, who did not appear to differentiate overmuch between getting into the beds of gentlemen or ladies, and whose fingers and tongue were quite amazingly adept...

After some thought Thomasina decided to invite Maud to Sunday lunch at Quire House. When they had eaten she would ask Maud to play some music for her – there was a piano in Quire's music room – and surely she could get through an hour or so of listening to some stuffy sonata.

The invitation would not be very remarkable, in fact it would be entirely in keeping with the Forrester tradition. Josiah Forrester had believed in showing consideration towards the people who worked for him, and he had taught his daughter to have the same sense of responsibility. Paternalism they called nowadays, he had said, but it was still plain old-fashioned consideration for dependents. Thomasina smiled as she remembered that her father had always been especially considerate to George Lincoln who had run the mill profitably and efficiently for so many years. The Miller of Twygrist, he used to say. That was George Lincoln, good faithful George. Pulled himself up by his bootstraps, of course – married money and learned how to be a gentleman as he went along – but none the worse for that.

After lunch on Sunday, Thomasina would take the miller's daughter for a walk in Quire's park, and then she would accompany Maud to her home. It would all be entirely chaste and perfectly respectable, although there would be a secret pleasure in walking close to Maud along the dark lanes, and slipping an arm around her waist to make sure she did not turn her ankle on an uneven piece of ground. It was unfortunate that the lane leading to the Lincolns' house lay alongside Latchkill – she frowned briefly over that – but they could hurry past the gates.

Chapter 16

Who Might Or Might Not Go To Your Main Character's Funeral?

WHY? It's early days, but perhaps that same childhood friend mentioned in the previous exercise, has become an enemy. Or stayed a loyal friend. This following exercise could open up some more possibilities.

Exercise

i)   Write a paragraph on 3 of these various connections who might go to your main character's funeral.

ii) Why?

iii) Write a paragraph on 3 who wouldn't.

iv) Why?

Examples

a) From my historical thriller, *Behold A Pale Horse*, currently being edited, where Catherine Ash comes home to her ambitious and bullying husband. Clement wouldn't go to her funeral because he'd be too busy looking after himself.

Nearing Moorgate tube station, Catherine could see that the choirmaster was still agitated by the way he snatched up the aerial on his battered Saab. She waved, but he turned away to force his key into the lock.

"Clement sends his regards." She shouted, and suddenly he spun round, mouth open. Then it melted to a smile, and she smiled too that she had calmedhim.

"Bloody cold," he said, getting in. He checked in the driving mirror. She was still there, the wife, but not yet mother, with the east wind teasing her golden mane around her head and blowing the day's debris into a dervish at her feet.

"Good news!" Clement Ash was home first, and behind the door the moment he'dheard her key. "Guess what?" His face with its shock of dark hair peered round the frame.

"Greenbaum's opening up in France, and he wants me to get the whole shebangon the road. My *Carte Professionelle* came through today..."

His large brown eyes seemed even more enormous, as though they belonged to someone else, and in his excitement, on hard, sprung calf muscles that never tired, bobbed up and down on the spot. Then he shut the door on her, almost trapping her foot.

"I won't let you in until you've said Wow! How wonderful and well done!"

Catherine sighed. It was one of those silly games again. But the cold wind was lashing her face. Tearing her raincoat away from her legs.

"Shit!"

"No, that won't do. Come on now. Say you're really, really pleased for me."

"I'm really, really pleased for you."

Catherine knew when to obey, seeing in an instant, like the moment before death, her whole life thrown into a kaleidoscopicspin.

"Well I think we can do better than that, don't you?" He was on a high. Unpredictable. Besides, the pavement behind her was deserted, for theirs was the only occupied house in the Chute Street docklands development. A narrow oasis of lit, uncurtained rooms, offering not comfort but fear.

Time was up.

"I think it's fantastic," she said. So he let her in. Fresh and strong in his flexitime lemon yellow tracksuit with a leaping gazelle appliquéd over his left breast.

"The *Carte de Séjour's* O.K too, so the old Jew wants me to be down thereready for the summer trade and all that."

"Where?"

b) From my in-progress thriller, *Lie of the Land* in which Shannon has been coerced by Marie into shoplifting. Now she's had enough.

2.20 p.m.

Shannon sighed at the last-minute change of plan. The Virgin Superstore was now first, just for the latest Adèle CD, nothing else. It was as if she didn't exist.

"Fuckin' amazing, it is," Marie pushed her way in with all the confidence of a seasoned 'lifter.' "You comin'?"

"I'm saving myself," lied Shannon. There weren't enough other punters. Marie would stand out too much. She scoured around for cameras then store detectives. She should warn her to stop looking over her shoulder all the time, but in her heart, she wanted her caught. Wanted out.

She slipped away into the sun-filtered arcade where, beyond its windows, a shimmering fountain seemed to spray the air with diamonds.

Chapter 17

Sexual Tension

Will they, won't they? A recipe for success.

Maxim Jakubowski writes best-selling erotic thrillers, and demand is strong.

A chiller thriller with no sexual tension is like a meal without flavoring. Most readers are female and you, the writer, might be leaving many of them disappointed without this all-too human element. The somewhat clichéd question, 'will they, won't they?' can be the gold thread developing through your narrative, adding richness and even more suspense to any plot.

Unless we have spent our adult lives shut away from the world, we have all experienced that first flicker of interest, the body language of someone who finds us attractive. The intensity of longing and the pleasure of gratification. In Graham Hurley's earlier political thrillers, his use of sexual tension enriches the often male-dominated scenarios and certainly kept many readers male and female, turning the pages.

As for describing the sex act, I'd only make this explicit if the manner of what's happening is important to the plot and if more is revealed about the participants' characters. Otherwise avoid what can seem like a rather gratuitous add-on.

Exercise
i)   Can you list 3 chiller thrillers produced in any medium, where the sexual tension has been memorable. Why?
ii) Consider two sex scenes and ask yourself if they were necessary or not.
iii) Write down candidly, your feelings when you first met someone who attracted you.
iv) Which of your chosen characters could form a sexual

relationship?

v) Would this last to the very end? If not, why?

vi) Could one of these characters betray the other? Or sacrifice their own life?

Important questions, but worth exploring.

Examples

a) From *Whittlewood* by Suzanne Ruthven, where attractive occultist Charlotte Manning is keeping the increasingly keen journalist, Alex Martin at arm's length.

Away from the motorway, a deep enveloping blackness swallowed the road and against the inky backdrop, skeletal branches stretched their bony arms towards the car as it raced past. Shortly after ten, the dim street lamps of the village gleamed like a beacon through the leafless hedgerow. Light drizzle glistened on the stonework as Alex swung the car under the archway and with a final roar the engine died in the cobbled courtyard. A dim gleam showed at the fanlight of the side door and before he had reached the step, a golden warmth flooded the gloom.

"You're just in time for supper," she calmly stated as he entered the narrow passageway.

All the resentment and anger faded at the sound of her voice. "You speak as though I were expected."

"You were."

She walked ahead of him into the lighted hallway, her lithe body concealed beneath a pale blue embroidered caftan. As she turned to take his coat, he was again surprised by her stature, barely reaching his shoulder in her bare feet. Gently, in spite of the urgency he felt, Alex took hold of her by the shoulders and pulled her towards him. As his mouth met hers for the first time, he held her close in a strangely familiar way, as though there had always been intimacy between them. The wanting that had consumed him was evident by the uncontrollable reaction of his body to the subtle caress of silk and fine perfume.

"So you sent for me and I came," he murmured into the darkness of her hair.

"Perhaps you are merely predictable," she replied coolly.

Her tart response broke the spell and he felt a certain inward relief as she calmly suggested they have supper. As always, Charlotte seemed to have him at a disadvantage. Did she *really* know that he was coming or was she merely quick witted enough to turn an unexpected situation to her advantage? However, supper for two *had* been set in the panelled alcove off the kitchen. The warmth from the huge blackened range seeped into his bones, as his unfathomable hostess ladled enormous helpings of homemade game soup into pottery bowls. The formality of his previous visit now comparing slightly less favourably with the present cosy atmosphere permeating the old kitchen.

b) From *Bloodstream* where plain, sixteen year-old English *au pair*, Pauline Archibald recalls a recent *rendezvous* with Jean-Marie Vincente, her employer's amoral brother, a top lawyer, who seduced her.

"Hey, Papa's place!" Solange had seen the long prefabricated building set amongst thinly planted poplars. There was no sign of the familiar silver Peugeot usually parked in the place reserved for '*le chef d'enterprise.*' Perhaps he had business elsewhere or a lunch with Jean-Marie whom he often met for legal advice, but now more frequently for the lifesaving trans-fusion of a loan. This lawyer was intimately acquainted with the minutiae of his brother's affairs, and party to all the adjustments that had changed '*La Toile d'Or*' from a prestigious silk producer - chief rival of Bucol in Lyon - to a manufacturer of household cottons.

But his name was all that Pauline could see coursing through her mind, encircling all other thoughts, just as the water of the river Bâtard eddied around its bristling reeds after a week of rain. A surge of longing gripped her every nerve, and her round white knees pressing into the coarse cloth of the seat in front, began to open. Heavy-jointed points of interest for the lawyer, a halfway house on his progress between her thighs. How she hated those formless mounds inherited from her mother, yet however hard she tried, they were always visible below her hem, whatever its length.

Dammit.

They were there now, beneath the half-drop repeat pattern of spring bluebells on her calf-length dress. A cringe-making reminder of that unreal encounter which every day, slipped irretrievably into the past.

As she tried to shift those well-worn images into a cohesive sequence, including the close-up detail of his handsome face and the line of his mouth, Frau Herrendorf braked violently behind an unsteady housewife on a bicycle, and Solange fell like a dead weight into her lap.

c) From *Behold A Pale Horse*, when Catherine Ash, abandoned near Collioure by her ambitious husband, is not unwillingly about to be seduced by Dr. Arnajon in his vegetable garden. A man with a dubious, dangerous past.

His canvas bag weighed heavily, all the more so to be clear of the ground. He was almost in the *Rue des Templiers* to deposit the herbs with his sister, when suddenly his heart leapt. Mrs. Ash was almost upon him, her cardigan loose around her shoulders like softly folded wings. This wasn't what he'd planned at all, but he composed himself sufficiently to block her way and reach into his bag. Thus the vegetable was between them, and Catherine stared as it lay quivering in his hand.

"Pour toi."

She looked round, cornered, and tried to sidestep into the road, but a hooting moped forced her back.

"It is chosen just for you."

For a brief moment he touched her arm, and his bleached eyes allowed her no escape as his thumbs gently parted the enclosing leaves. "Look. *Volkommen.*" He thrust it forwards. This was foliage not skin. A crown of florettes, not gristled head. No dreadful fear. She took it and thanked him politely.

"I have more," he said. "Many more. In my garden of Eden there is something of everything."

Catherine then noticed his wide gold ring. "Your wife must be pleased, then."

He was silent, and then in that awkward void, she suddenly realised he was the man she'd seen in the old photograph. Although time had coarsened and eroded those prosperous looks, the gaze remained unchanged. She was held, like the flies on the butcher's syrupy strips, unable to tear away.

"Would you like to see this Paradise?" He asked, and she saw how it was only his tongue that moved, appearing and disappearing between his lips. Reptilian and shiny from its dry skin cave. "It will give you much pleasure *je te garanti.*"

There was no obvious reason to resist for every second now seemed to draw her away from her other existence on an ever-quickening tide.

Chapter 18

Pecking Order

You're the boss. Or are you?

Deciding on a pecking order helps to avoid lesser, walk-on parts possibly developing a bigger life of their own and taking over in a way that could risk cluttering/derailing your plot, however hazy or certain it is at the start.

Exercise

Create your cast list in order of importance. At this stage, don't get too complicated!

Later on, if - as in my *Malediction* - you end up with a large cast of characters, a full list at the beginning of your book is very useful to the reader. Especially where some have pseudonyms.

Examples

a) Character list from *Malediction*. This might seem like a lot, but there are just nine who are the most significant and were in place early on. I admit that only as late as two thirds of the way through, was I able to organize the rest!

MALEDICTION

Dramatis Personae

Colette Bataille: mother of Bertrand *aka Sister Barbara*.
Bertrand Bataille: her son, *aka Le Bébé*.
Nelly Augot: her new-found friend, *aka Yveline*.
Guy Baralet: Director of Medex. Colette's boss.
Lise Baralet: his wife. A florist.
Robert Vidal: Father Jean-Baptiste of La Sainte Vièrge in Lanvière-sur-Meuse Colette's lover.

Francke Duvivier: Father André of St Trinité in Les Pradels, Provence. *Aka* Thibaut/*Kommandant*/*Haupsturmführer.*

Michel Plagnol: Father Jérome of Notre Dame de la Consolation in Drancy, Paris. *aka* The Pigface

Éric Cacheux: Father Christophe de la Bonté of St.Honoré in the Corbières.

Dominique Mathieu: Father Xavier-Marie of La Motte Mauron in Perros Guirec.

Christian Désespoir: Abbot of Legrange Vivray, founder of Les Pauvres Soeurs de la Souffrance.

René Martin: Deacon of Les Bourreux

Raôul Bourra: Bishop of Kervecamp

Henri Pereire: Bishop of Beauregard

Philippe Toussirot: Dominican Bishop of Ramonville

Georges Déchaux: General with NATO peace-keeping forces. *Aka Hauptsturmbannführer for the ACJ.*

Nina Zeresche: police switchboard operator.

Antoinette Ruffiac: *aka Claude Lefêbvre. Receptionist at St Anne's hostel/Déchaux's chauffeur in Paris.*

Christine Souchier: *aka Romy Kirchner/ 'ma souris rouge.' Also at hostel.*

Giselle Subradière: *aka Simone Haubrey/Patrice Sassoule*

Marie-Claude Huron: temp at Medex (where Colette worked) *aka Julie Borel*

Sister Agnes: recruiting nun for Les Pauvres Soeurs.

Sister Marie-Ange: Sister Superior

Sister Cecilia: the Inquisitor. *aka 'le Percheron.'*

Sister Rose: Cleaner

Yves Jalibert: ACJ co-ordinator in Paris.

Marcel Jalibert: his son.

Mordecai Fraenkel: hotelier at the King David Hotel near the Loire.

Pauline Fraenkel: his wife.

Leila Fraenkel: their daughter. An artist.

Michèle Bauer-Lutyens: receptionist at the King David Hotel.

b) Michael Jecks is the author of many successful mediaeval historical thrillers including the latest, *King's Gold*. Here is not only a full list of characters from Sir Baldwin de Furnshill, clever investigator and Keeper of the King's Peace, to Squire Bernard, a porter at Kenilworth Castle's gate, but also a comprehensive Glossary. All adding to the reader's understanding and inclusion in the story.

Chapter 19

Nature v Nurture? What Makes Your Main Characters Tick?

That people don't change, they just reveal themselves, seems to be so true. Yet there are exceptions. For example, it was reported recently that a petty thief became a vicious armed robber when he developed a brain tumor. That a woman developed serious OCD (Obsessive compulsive disorder) after receiving a heart transplant.

But let's go back...

Sometimes, those of us who are parents, look at our child and wonder 'where did you come from?' Indeed, in cases of mass murder and other heinous crimes, the perpetrator has often come from a loving, apparently normal home, which makes their actions all the more inexplicable. Perhaps, criminality is an affliction divorced from anything else, and yet as a writer who's considering your reader, I feel that if you've created such a character, even the smallest clue as to their evil is helpful.

Conversely, someone brought up in the most dismal, brutish surroundings can grow up to be generous and kind, making those around them immediately feel better. People are complicated, which is why some study of psychology can be enormously helpful when it's your characters driving the storyline.

'There's nowt so queer as folk,' is another apt saying, and without space here to identify all the permutations of human behavior, one aspect is topical. This cyber age is peopled by loners who move around the internet concealing their real identity. Whatever they say or do cannot be directly linked to the rest of their lives. Their toxic disinhibition can however, ruin others' lives and reputations. These surfers are invisible and dangerous. A gift for the chiller thriller writer where you can manipulate your reader into having a sneaking hope that villains such as these, escape justice. Far more subversive than willing your warts-and-all hero/ine to survive. But whether you're creating beasts or angels, your reader must care *about* them, not necessarily *for* them.

Exercises

i) What might have shaped your main characters? E.g; their genetic inheritance and early experiences, including religion.

ii) How have they changed since they were young children?

iii) What possible event/s might have changed them? (Think of Clarice Starling's youthful trauma)

iv) What are their goals?

v) What could stand in their way?

vi) Their obsession/s?

vii) Their Achilles heel?

viii) Who do they love?

ix) Are they to be trusted? (All too often, we have come to trust those who would harm us the most. And a few years ago in Italy, a killer nurse kept a secret diary of her crimes against her patients, admitting that killing them gave her a sense of power. Secret, sibling rivalry is also dangerous.)

x) Can they be manipulated?

xi) Are they reckless?

Examples

a) From my historical Gothic chiller, *The Yellowhammer's Cradle* where we meet the pretty, hard-done-by Catriona McPhee who has recently killed her father's wealthy lover. I want the reader to feel pity for her. To wish her well with her dreams. And yet she is dangerous.

I.

14th January 1847

Where blood is thinner than water...

Although Christmas, the New Year and Feast of the Epiphany, had all passed in a blur of windless drizzle - or smirr, as the locals called it – and even thirteen year-old Catriona McPhee knew Argyll was no longer a place for the sick or faint-hearted. For seven long days and nights, Atlantic gales had pounded its mountains, forests and lochs, severing trees and destroying all but the most sturdy of dwellings. So far, the McPhee's but and ben had survived, for Footer's Hill had shielded their two-roomed hovel from the westerly blast. Even so, water tumbled down its bracken-covered sides, flooding the nearby hill loch, turning her father Iain's once cultivated plot into a treacherous bog.

Her mother said the Devil was at work in a Godless land, and her daughter must therefore lay her innocent hand on the Bible and offer up a prayer for their continued deliverance. Her father, for his part, blamed Lord Melhuish whose brutal Clearance for sheep grazing, had ended his job as herdsman, leaving him to beg for the three of them to stay on in this pitiful shack until he found new employment at the next Feeing Fair.

With nowhere else to go, and a prisoner of growing tension between her parents, Catriona soon withdrew into her dreams. All the while, the mad wind whistled down the chimney, making the fire spit out wet wood, bringing a draught through every stone to torment the one candle and turn her blood to ice. Such storms made any outdoor life impossible. No walks to Cranranich to meet girls of her own age, or to peep at the huge, impenetrable Ardnasaig House on the shore of Loch Nonach. The one wonder of her own small world. But at least the weather had prevented her last Kirk visit with her mother to endure yet another dreary sermon on the wicked ways of men; surely a blessing in itself.

Now, with each bleak hour that passed, she observed the cracks in her parents' marriage growing wider. Perhaps if she'd had a brother or sister, they could have invented different homes complete with servants to fetch them freshly baked dainties topped by colored icing. To warm their sheets on beds hung with silk, and dress them in the kind of clothes that only the very rich could afford from shops in Edinburgh and Glasgow. Although her mother's three late miscarriages meant these fairytales remained unshared.

Mairi McPhee longed for a better life for them all. A Kirk minister's daughter from Tarbet, she'd married for love and the chance to escape her strict Presbyterian home. But Iain McPhee's sudden, humiliating loss of work last June, changed her into a hermit, never mixing with her former women friends, or bothering with her appearance. Her pale hair had turned silver. Her frame thinned from slender to skin and bone. Her skin dry and pitted.

"Look at him." She angled her pinched face towards the struggling fire, where the once fit and handsome man lolled in his chair, open-mouthed. "Sleep, sleep, sleep. All he ever does," she wheezed. "And while he rests his lazy bones, what are we supposed to live on?"

Catriona had long given up having ideas for him to make money. Besides, who'd employ a man so wedded to the heavy, he was rarely out of bed before midday?

"Why not sell Bibles for the Kirk?" She suggested to her mother. "Or all those other books you've kept for so long?"

"Without them my soul would break. They're the cure for all his pagan blasphemy. Remember when I dared have you Christened last autumn? He was quite happy to see you spin in Hell when your time comes."

This effort made her clasp her chest, draw her breath in rusty, agonizing gasps. A fresh blast of rain battered the one small window so hard, Catriona waited for the breaking of glass. And still her father slept. Still God wasn't listening. She shivered, watching Mairi McPhee shuffle to the window and press both palms against the trembling pane as if to stop it shattering. However, if she was honest, her father's unbelief was far more interesting than her mother's rigid faith.

"You must raise yourself out of the mire." Her mother, this time barely whispering. "I've given you a good education here so you can leave and better yourself whichever way you can."

b) From David Evans's gripping second thriller, *Torment*, set in Wakefield, where Chris waits for brother Gary to return to their car. His tone is of regret, but danger lurks…

Dropping the window a touch, he lit a cigarette and tried to relax. A half moon gave a little light but clouds kept sweeping across and pitching the scene into darkness every now and then.

He was growing increasingly uncomfortable thinking about the events of the past few months. What started out as being a means to an end, a one-off to avoid any embarrassment, had become a burden. He had told himself he was helping Gary but that was far from the truth. It was bringing him back into crime again. And all because of his weakness. If he hadn't spotted the advert; if he hadn't looked for it in the first place. If he hadn't walked in through the door. And Mariana, she drew him in, hook line and sinker. Unlike her, he shouldn't have used his real name, shouldn't have told her anything about himself, what he did, where he worked. If he hadn't, none of this would have happened. He would never have been drawn into the whole murky world of car crime.

He never spotted the car come in behind and stop about twenty yards from his. The lights were already off when it left the main road. A figure in dark clothes and wearing a balaclava stepped silently from the car. The figure watched the smoke escape from the driver's window, then looked to the sky. Clouds were just about to cover the moon once more, and for a considerable time. The figure waited until the moonlight had gone before making his way towards Baker's Rover, pausing to screw the silencer tube to the gun barrel.

Baker drew on his cigarette for the last time. As he flicked the butt from the window, his periphery vision caught a slight movement. It was the last thing he would ever be conscious of. A low crack, then his brains were churned into soup inside his skull. The lifeless body slumped forward, head on the steering wheel, arms down by its side.

The figure turned and walked away from the car, removing the silencer as he went.

Down in the ditch, Gary had finished and was desperately trying for a foothold to get himself back up to the fence. Finally, he managed to grab hold of the bottom rail and pull himself up the last few feet, just in time to see a car drive out of the lay-by and back onto the main road, waiting until the last moment to put the lights on. "Bollocks," he said to himself. "I've missed the handover."

Climbing back over the fence he scraped as much mud off his shoes as he could. He didn't want to upset his brother any more.

"I suppose you laughed your bollocks off when I went over that fence," he said, approaching the car. "Chris? What the fuck are you fiddling about with down there?" Altering course, he walked up to the driver's door and opened it. "Come on," he said, giving his brother a shake. The corpse rolled to one side and half fell out.

He gasped. "Oh Christ. Oh Jesus fucking Christ."

c) In my psychological thriller, *Overspill*, another work being edited, set in Coventry's London overspill slums and a contrasting gated development, the murderous, damaged Louis Perelman, gifted violinist, is a beautiful looking boy with a sweet smile. No wonder Rita Martin who lives on the wrong side of the tracks, is worried about his growing influence over her son. And here, Louis is out to play…

I.

Saturday 2nd July.

The heat makes everything bubble. His skin, his scalp under his fine brown hair and the lenses of his glasses, but worst of all, the stagnant malodorous pool grown from the brook which meanders south through three housing estates until it reaches the Oxford Canal.

The schoolboy sets down his blazer then his violin case which to him seems shaped like some weird coffin. Even the domed darkness around him appears ripe for death. Not his own, however, for that's a subject which has never engaged him.

Now beech and alder conspire to shut out the sky, to keep this place secret from prying eyes, condensing the vapours from decades of rotting leaves and the human effluent which lies beneath the water's skin.

He can hear his new watch. The one *they* got him for his birthday. The Fawn and The Maggot. People he can manipulate for his own ends. People who, since he was able to understand such things have denied him his ultimate craving. To know who he is. Who made him…

All at once the lad lets out a cry of excitement for the little waterborne family is on time. He and his new friend who is habitually late have kept a log of their daily arrivals, particularly since the cygnets were hatched. As always, mother swan swims first followed by her three *things* dipping their scraggy necks into the sludge, nervously eyeing the bank, before sudden surges to catch up.

"Hello runt." He stares at the last in line. The boy had found that word in his dictionary and likes saying it whenever he can, and now here's the creature in real life, flesh and blood, lagging conveniently behind, half the size of the other two - the last to share in any pickings.

First his stone lands on target. Next he rips a branch from a tree - its forked end perfect for bringing in the harvest...The runt is heavier than expected, its noise the oddest thing he's ever heard. Into the undergrowth then, its terrified eyes lined with stuff like plasticine, squeezing tight...

Crack...

The next bit never lets him down. The leather-sheathed knife he'd found in its usual place makes everything easy peasy. Grey feathers everywhere in the peeling, floating without landing...

He has help now for his friend has arrived, out of breath but keen to show off his new butchering skills. Then afterwards, with the bloodied bird thrown back into the brook and sinking, they compare penises. Use a twig to measure their excitement. But because of no foreskin, the violinist's erection is the shorter and in that brief moment his brittle pleasure vanishes, leaving only shame and hurt which lingers all the way home.

Chapter 20

Why?

Your biggest question.

This needs exploring in some detail, because without believable MOTIVATIONS, your characters won't be convincing. Why will your main protagonist set out to identify and fight the perceived evil? What does it threaten?

Secondly, another simple question. *Why* might their enemy be obstructive? Destructive? Depraved?

Only in rare cases do people perpetrate terrible acts for no apparent reason, as if they exist in a vacuum. Most have a trigger from somewhere. Main motives for harm against others are; Envy; Revenge; Greed; Rivalry; Betrayal; Loss (in its widest sense).

For your readers, there has to be a WHY? To avoid this question gives you a story resembling a boneless body.

Exercises

i) Identify at least 3 other characters' motives in at least 2 published chiller thrillers. You'll find this useful.

ii) Explore your own main protagonist's motivations. Even if at some point, they collude in what they are investigating or fighting. Double agents have been amongst us forever.

iii) Explore his/her enemy's motivation for what they have done/are doing/will do. This has to ring true, and deep down you'll know if you're fudging it!

Examples

a) Gerald Seymour's Mafia thriller, *Killing Ground* has tragic characters a-plenty, tense interactions and a steadily building storyline. Its main protagonist, Charley Parsons is a young British schoolteacher who four years before, was nanny to a wealthy Sicilian family's children. She finds herself convinced to go back to them to be used as bait by the American Drug enforcement Agency to trap her employer. The next head of the Sicilian Mafia. I'd need to know what convinced her to do this, and will she betray him?

b) In *Silence of the Lambs*, FBI trainee, Clarisse Starling is determined to unravel Hannibal Lecter - an utterly original baddie - who can even smell her as she walks by his cell. Instead of imparting what he knows of current sadistic serial killer, 'Buffalo Bill,' he'd rather dwell on her Achilles heel by making her re-live a traumatic event from her youth. As an orphan she was sent to relatives in Montana where she tried and failed to save a lamb from their slaughterhouse. This tragic failure has never left her.

A very believable example of how an event others might consider trivial, has tainted this conscientious young woman's life.

Chapter 21

Time For Adventure!

The Timeslip possibility.

I have always enjoyed and indeed looked out for crime and thriller fiction where different time-frames are used in the narrative. However, excluding the TV drama series, *Life on Mars*, the historical thriller, *Lady of Hay*, and the creepy, suburban home in *House of Leaves*, which shifts to the Mesolithic era, convincing examples seem rare.

Yet judging by the spontaneous responses of those attending my talks and workshops, I'm not alone in having experienced this unbidden occurrence. To date, all mine have happened in or near the French Pyrenees.

Once my Dutch aunt had explained how our antecedents had fled Spain during the Spanish Inquisition and come through these mountains to the Low Countries, did my odd experiences begin to make sense. Why, for example, I couldn't take the family into the Grotte de Lombrives, a popular tourist attraction near Tarascon in the Ariège department, because I'd suddenly felt a crippling claustrophobia and had begged to be driven away from that dark opening as quickly as possible. She later claimed, some of the unlucky escapees had been walled up inside.

Again, on a narrow road leading north east from Rennes le Château towards the village of Bugarach and its supposedly significant mountain, I slipped away from my husband into what seemed a weirdly familiar past. The same sensation as whenever I go to the silent, almost secretive village of Montaillou. However, what's strange about that same narrow road, is that not until eight years later, did I realize that the house we eventually bought and have kept for almost twenty-four years, connected directly to it via the Gorges de Galamus some forty kilometers away.

Even Proust in his *À la recherche du temps perdu*, writes of his experience "… of having before me, inserted in the present actual hour, a little of the past, that dreamlike impression which one experiences in Venice on the Piazetta before its two columns of grey and pink granite… and who both, without understanding the conversations going on around them in a language that is not of their country, on this public square… keep on prolonging our midst their days of the twelfth century, of the twelfth century long since vanished, springs up a double light thrust of pink granite. All around, the actual days, the days we are living, circulate, rush buzzing around the columns, but suddenly stop there; flee like repelled bees; for those high and slender enclaves of the past are not in the present, but in another time where the present is forbidden to penetrate."

I've been amazed at how many of my audiences and writing students almost eagerly, volunteered their own experiences of this phenomenon in all kinds of different places. Why some have explored the subject further, also enjoying the historical novels of writers such as Barbara Erskine who so vividly, almost magically, re-create bygone worlds far removed from their own. Her first chiller, *Lady of Hay* has few equals. In it, Jo Clifford, a successful journalist, cynical of past-life regression, undergoes hypnosis and begins to re-live the tragic life of Matilda of Hay, some eight hundred years before. Both this idea and the more spontaneous experience of the timeslip, offer you, the chiller thriller writer, huge possibilities.

The transmigration of souls, where at death, the released soul finds an empty womb to inhabit, be it human or animal, is one of the main tenets of Catharism. A fascinating notion. My own view is that although I personally sense I've been round the block before, we don't really 'know' anything for certain.

Exercises
i)   Have you experienced any sense of a timeslip? Either

forwards or backwards, where a place you'd never been to before, or a person you'd never met before, seemed familiar?

ii) Have you ever, under hypnosis or regression, felt you were someone else? Somewhere else?

Examples

a) Read the remarkable, non-fiction book *Adventures in Time* by Andrew MacKenzie, details many accounts from 'ordinary' people who've seen 'vanished' buildings, found themselves in distant eras such as three servicemen in the Suffolk village of Kersey on a mediaeval Sunday morning, and others in a cottage-lined Nottingham street now lined with factories. Not to be missed!

b) Check out *Strangers* by Taichi Yamada. A paranormal, slow-burn thriller set in Japan, now being made into a film. The dream-like sequences with the main characters' long-dead parents who seem to have come alive and live in the present, contrasts with the push and shove of urban Japanese life.

c) From my chiller, *The Fold*, where ineffectual French teacher, Suzanne Price, recognises the Madonna which the secretive Pierre Arties is carving in front of his hovel in Siguerac. The telegraph wires are significant because they will soon connect the present to a deadly past.

"I bought three identical carvings in Lavelenet," she ventured. "I might be wrong... " She tailed off at his silence, for there was nothing more to add in the cold detachment that descended between indigene and interloper.

"You are all wrong." He said.

She noticed how telephone wires connected to his crumbling chimney quivered, emptying of summer birds, and in that moment, felt no warmth from the sun. Instead, the low, threatening pain she'd experienced before the journey, had returned, sapping her earlier confidence and camaraderie.

A feeling of inexplicable dread and desolation gripped her under that holiday-brochure sky, as she followed the fragrant hedgerow which overlooked the summery fields and the serenity of distant country.

Directly ahead, she could see that the minibus had arrived and the student was encircling the waiting group with a loop of loud music from the stereo. An arm dangled casually out of the window, fingers drumming against the yellow door. He was in no hurry to come to a halt and cruised tantalisingly around the parking area several times before the dogs in their wide hawthorn collars lunged at his hand.

"Please stop!" she bleated. "We have to get back as soon as possible!" She knew they'd all stayed too long, and his foot indolently on the accelerator, was delaying their escape. "We have luggage to collect, things to organise... "

But he'd pulled away yet again, turning up the volume until the silent centre of Siguerac reverberated to heavy metal. *God on the Rocks.*

She ran after him, inhaling the exhaust, making no effort to call off the mastiffs whilst her colleague oblivious to her distress, stretched upwards under the trees, defoliating the lower branches. With both dogs tenaciously clinging to the door, the driver was forced to pull in and amidst deafening noise the group climbed inside.

"I'll be reporting this tomorrow, make no mistake." She stood over him, breasts heaving under the downy clinging wool of her jumper.

But Pierre Arties and his brother-in-law, without the inconvenience of having to wait for transport, or of finding the correct money for connection to a foreign telephone exchange, were able to do that much more easily.

Chapter 22

Who'll Tell The Story?

New writers emerging from Degree and Post-Graduate creative writing courses, keen to make their mark, seem more and more to use the multi-viewpoint and different tenses in their first novels as if to create a deliberate patchwork effect. Experimentation is fine – one only has to look at *House of Leaves* - but your reader mustn't feel defeated. The success or not of your chiller thriller depends upon having the strongest, most involving character or characters delivering the goods, and keeping the reader engaged.

So, will you choose an omniscient voice throughout? Or that of a sole protagonist or the world and his wife? Think carefully before giving anyone other than your main protagonist a viewpoint. They will have to maintain the suspense, reveal and react to things of which the main protagonist isn't necessarily aware. They'll need secrets too...

There are several different points of view (POV) for you to consider;

1st person POV. E.g; The elevator took me to the 30th floor from where I could see the Hudson River far below, lit up like a silver ribbon.

2nd person POV. E.g; You never waited for your thesis on Verlaine to be returned, instead you pushed past the professor of French and ran across to the quadrangle gate.

3rd person limited POV. E.g; Melissa Grove sits, knees tightly crossed, fingers locking and unlocking until a man's voice calls out her name.

No, I can't...

Fear has frozen every part of her, yet all the while, she sees his shadow drawing closer.

3ʳᵈ person omniscient POV. Max leant out of the open window feeling dizzy, swaying on his bare feet. Julia stared at his tanned back knowing that in the next few seconds, he'd be turning round. Her best friend would see to that.

Epistolatory form – a POV delivered solely by means of letters, faxes, texts or emails. *It's Time We Talked About Kevin*, used this intriguing device, which, can in less clever hands, distance the reader from the action.

In my Introduction, I've already mentioned the author's device of using an unreliable narrator, and here's your opportunity. Doctor Shepard in Agatha Christie's *The Murder of Roger Ackroyd*, although not a thriller, is nevertheless a brilliant example of fooling the reader.

Exercises

i) Who could be *your* unreliable narrator?

ii) Examine several chiller thrillers by visiting any bookshop or library. Or sample or buy a work displayed online to see how other writers use this ploy; also, either single or different viewpoints.

iii) Why should any other of your characters be heard? What have they to say? To reveal?

  Unless their cupboard's full, you'll soon run out of steam with them.

Examples

3ʳᵈ person limited POV.

a)Throughout *A Night With No Stars*, we hear not only main protagonist Lucy Mitchell's 'voice' but also those of the two strange, quite different brothers, Mark and Richard Jones who, chapter by chapter, sway the reader from believing one then the other. I wanted to create uncertainty as to which of these two was a vicious killer. Here, in chapter 2, Richard, with the third person limited POV, is about to leave Sydney and come home. He's been in exile too long...

2.

While Lucy was back in her Tooting flat, sluicing away Benn's legacy under her antediluvian shower, some ten hours ahead of GMT and 12,000 miles away in Sydney, former bank clerk Robert Ferris Barker clamped a nervy hand on his alarm clock the moment its wake-up call began. He'd set it for 11pm the night before, knowing he wouldn't sleep a wink with the racket going on in the unit next door. He decided it wasn't worth having a blue over it. Not with what he'd got planned for the next 24 hours.

He blinked out at the eerie night sky which cast his old roller blind a strange silvery colour, and if he moved his head just a little, he could see the ivory disc of a full moon hover over Redfern's tenement blocks. There was something about it which stirred his memory and made him swing his tanned legs off the mattress with more vigour than anything he'd recently done at work. He switched on the shadeless bulb which hung from the ceiling by a knotted black flex, peed into the small cracked hand basin, then washed himself thoroughly all over with the tepid water which came one-paced from the single lime-scaled tap.

He checked himself in the mirror nailed over the sink. He looked okay, he thought, considering, and decided to leave the three days' stubble on his chin. In fact, every guy who was someone in Sydney was doing the same. Besides, it made him look older which was no bad thing.

Having doused himself with Urgent, a leaving present from the sheilas at the bank, he dressed in his work clothes and the expensive trenchcoat which he always kept in a dry clean wrap behind the door. That way he'd come over as a guy on business or a lawyer even, especially with his briefcase and matching luggage kindly donated by his boss and the Senior Team.

He checked his travel documents yet again. He'd been systematic about all of that, but at some cost to his recent social life. However, it was worth it and nothing was now more pleasurable than to safely re-tuck the white-smile photos, the proof of his dual nationality and return visa into their special pale pigskin wallet. Next he counted out all the pounds sterling he'd saved since last March; since his decision to shake off a life of forever looking over his shoulder; suspicious of strangers and the secrets behind their eyes. Why he'd shacked up in Redfern in the first place. It was a cesspit, but had suited his need for anonymity. He'd lived cheap, walked to the bank on Upper Street which kept him fit and where he could shower, and now it was time to say adios.

b) From *Dark Harvest*, the third in my DI Martin Webb thriller trilogy, where his friend Chris Mears, lost in the Queensland outback, is thinking about the past.

Five.
Tuesday 25th July 23.35hrs. EST.

A silent world, muffled by sand that had settled in every part of him. Every orifice, every hollow, it seemed.

"Born asleep." Wasn't that's what his newborn baby brother's grave in Blackheath had said? James Richard Mears. 23rd May 1983, beloved infant son of Pamela and Peter Mears. Never again to be spoken of since the funeral. Would the same happen to him when he was gone? He who'd had the luck of a good pair of lungs, a stronger heart with normal rhythm, but unending guilt that it had been so. Would his mother clam up again, as if by not uttering "Christopher Peter Mears," she could pretend he'd never struggled from her body? Yes, struggled, according to her and his doting godmother whenever the two had met. How, like that of his dead brother, the umbilical cord had wound itself tighter and tighter around his neck as he'd emerged from the birth canal unable to breathe.

But here was worse, because he'd known life, friendship, love, and wasn't yet ready to give it all up. When he'd first heard the *Horizon* advancing through the sand, he'd assumed it was Angelica at its wheel, come looking for him. But if so, why hadn't she called out, even if just to curse him for leaving her? And how the Hell had she got hold of another spare key?

Too late now to worry about all that. He'd picked himself up where he'd fallen in the headlights' yellow pools, abandoned the bike and, aware of the yelps of nearby wild dogs, had thrown himself into what future he still had. Not daring to look back while a deep inner sense - the kind Martin Webb once claimed he possessed - urged him to push ahead, however impossible that was proving.

The wind had risen to beyond gale force, hurling sand against his unprotected head. He closed his eyes and stumbled forwards, knee-deep, thigh deep. Anything rather than fall again. Just like during that Offa's Dyke trip when he and Webby had been chased by two loose cows. Only his best mate's encouragement had spared him a trampling. Now, all those years later, he could still hear his shouts in his clogged-up ears.

"Go on, go on, Chris. You can do it!"

And just then, the headlights that had harassed him for too long, finally faded and died.

Different lights now, twinkling from across the water along the mainland's beach.

At bloody last.

With that hopeful sign ahead of him, and the smell of the sea intensifying, the deep sand underfoot seemed to thin out and the wild dog noise dissolve into the night. But surely these better conditions would also be enabling his pursuer to make progress? He could hear the *Horizon's* engine picking up, its inadequate wheels grumbling over the ups and downs of the uneven terrain. If it wasn't Angelica at the helm, then who?

Chapter 23

What's The Outline?

In a nutshell. Getting the show on the road.

An outline is not a blurb. (More on that later.) It's a working summary of your proposed story for you to keep in mind once you begin your chiller thriller. See it as a coat hanger on which to hang your fleshed-out theme. It may, by the end, be irrelevant, but it's a useful start.

Exercise

In approximately 50 words, write the bare bones, giving them room to breathe...

Examples

a) A sample idea.

In 2007, a happily-married couple in their forties, move from London to Vermont, USA where the husband has taken up a dream job with a newspaper. He discovers an unsolved case from 1975 when a famous jazz player and his pilot vanished while on an internal flight to a gig. One day, there's a knock on the door. This stranger comes with news that could destroy everything.

b) My Outline for *The Leper House.*

July 1920, and Will Parminter and his young family are forced to leave the New Forest after his frightening brush with death. They eventually arrive in rural Norfolk, in a heat wave, desperate for work. In November 1988, ex-DI John Lyon goes to stay in that same area with a former university friend – now a married history professor - who despite threats, cover-ups in the highest places, and murder, is determined to find the truth about their fate.

Chapter 24

Plotting

Most of us learnt in school that a good story needs a beginning, middle and end. To this basic skeleton can be added a Prologue, a sub-plot or two, a climax and an Epilogue.

When men, women and children first crouched in caves and stories and legends were shared, nobody present would have sat around long enough to listen to something that literally left them cold. Like today's readers, listeners and viewers, they wanted to be lifted from their day-to-day world to something far more exciting.

This should be your goal when you sit down to write, and the more you immerse yourself as a reader within the thriller genre, the more you'll identify the best and worst examples. Rejoice in the best, but remember the worst so you don't make those same mistakes. Character-driven plots will always linger for longer in the reader's mind than plot-driven stories. Even if, in the remarkable case of *House of Leaves*, the main character is the house.

Since those long-ago days when literary v genre didn't exist, there have always been three basic plots.

i) Relationships.

Which can reach a point of implosion or explosion.

ii) The Uninvited Guest.

This universal threat can be interpreted in so many ways. In *Stoker*, a recent dark thriller film, it's Uncle Charlie who purrs up to Evelyn Stoker and her daughter's mansion in Nashville. In *Cold Remains*, it's the demanding, unquiet spirit of Margiad Pitt-Rose who brings danger.

iii) A Quest.

Think Dan Brown with *The Da Vinci Code*; Ian Fleming with 007. Think where *you're* going.

Back to the collective unconscious and what most people are most scared of. This doesn't mean you are all going to write about being buried alive, or a beloved only child snatched in a super-market. But our fear and your fear will underpin what you embark upon.

For me, the Dutch author, Tim Krabbé's *The Vanishing*, ticks every chiller thriller box. It begins with such hope and optimism. I'm not going to spoil things by revealing the plot, but would urge you to read the novel and see the film, of which there are several versions.

I hope this and your other reading will show you the way.

Exercises

i) Wikipedia show quite detailed plots of both well-known chiller thriller books and films. Worth a read. Also Amazon and other selling/review sites.

ii) I'd also recommend you read *The Whicker Man*, by the late Anthony Shaffer, twin of Peter. In it, Sergeant Howie, based on the Scottish mainland, receives an anonymous letter asking him to come to a remote Hebridean island to search for the young Rowan Morrison, missing for a number of months. He's a devout and celibate Christian who's shocked to find a society that worships the pagan Celtic gods of their ancestors, encourages outdoor sex and every other sin. Again, I won't give the ending away, but the whole premise is truly shocking.

As for redemption – what redemption?

iii) Working from your outline, try more detailed plotting. The journey from A to B with possible sub-plots. (See the next chapter for more detail.) Let your characters steer the boat and you keep your lifebelt handy!

iv) You may by now have read or are reading *House of Leaves*. Can you identify its two plotlines?

v) Do they work for you?

Chapter 25

Structuring

There are various ways of structuring your chiller thriller to create the most exciting reading experience. It is tempting to follow the herd and stick to the perceived rules. However, there has to be room for invention and courage, and in 2000, American author, Mark Z. Danielewski blazed the trail.

His 700 page long *House of Leaves* is a chiller about a book which is in turn about a video of video-journalist Will Navidson and his young family who move into a physics-defying house like no other. Using footnotes, the unloveable narrator, Johnny Truant tells the story of blind Zampano who left a trunk full of notes called the Will Navidson Records. These include cryptic graphs, strange photographs and drawings. It's believed that the book's unique structure may have been inspired by *The Raw Shack Texts* by Stephen Hall. I can't comment on that, but suffice it to say, this esoteric chiller has it all.

The most successful thrillers usually include the following four components;

I. LAYERING

Past, present and future? Or all three?

Layering is a popular device which can involve contemporaneous action in one or two or more totally different settings. Or historically, involving another era, characters and event/s from the past. Or futuristically. Yes, you'll have to keep your eye on the ball, but ultimately, your chiller thriller will be richer and even more suspenseful as these important layers ultimately shape its climax and ending.

2. A SUB PLOT

or two can help avoid an over-linear storyline, so try and identify a possible scenario to bubble beneath or alongside your main narrative until affecting the climax and ending. Remember, over-complicated plotting can land you and your characters in the mire. 'Less is more' is a useful dictum.

The best way to understand the sub-plot, is to read a well-reviewed contemporary thrillers and discover what else is happening apart from the main story. For example, supposing your main character has a younger brother who's behaving oddly. As the days go by, he becomes more weird. More difficult to reach. Why? How might this affect the climax and ending?

Exercises

i)   Identify a published chiller thriller in which layering occurs using one or more different eras and characters to create its main plot.

ii) Did this work for you? Try and analyse your 'yes' or 'no.'

iii) Identify any sub plots.

iv) Did these convince you?

v)   Create your own sub plot by using a complete stranger or one of your main character's connections from another era, to add to the suspense of your climax and ending.

vi) Can you recognise another possible sub-plot opportunity in your book? It may be staring you in the face!

vii) What extra research will you need to do?

Examples

a) *Spider Light* by Sarah Rayne, draws upon both the late Victorian era and the near present day, in which the actions of the devious Thomasina Forrester and her connections in the past, cause tragedy to affect the present..

b) In *Cold Remains* set in 2009, my first sub-plot concerns dedicated headmaster, Lionel Hargreaves, who, back in 1946 is running the village school and asking too many questions, The second, in 2009 brings troubled thug, Llyr Pitt-Rose on to the scene. His secret story has stayed stays buried until surfacing half way through with his own POV, and ends just before this chiller's climax.

3. SHORT CHAPTERS

Not all thriller writers use the time-honoured format of dividing their work into chapters. There are other exciting and perfectly acceptable substitutes which you could consider. Perhaps a quotation from a character foreshadowing events. Sections from some ancient, imagined document. Images, such as appeared on photographic film during the Scole Experiment. However, if you do decide to use chapters, keep them short.

This is nothing to do with the notion that our attention span might be diminishing daily, but that the essential element of a good thriller is pace. Keeping your chapters short, and ending each with the reader gasping to know what happens next. Any chapter over 20 pages long, risks losing the tension.

Remember how the American TV drama *24* starring Kiefer Sutherland had hourly chunks of non-stop action? Each ending with a cliff-hanger? This was literally thrilling viewing.

Exercises

i) What possible alternatives to the traditional chapter can you devise?

ii) See what other writers, even of Fantasy and Science Fiction have done.

iii) Check the number of chapter pages that recently published thriller writers use.

iv) Did you prefer those books where there was some variation in length?

v) Were the chapters too long? Too short?

Example

In my ex-DI John Lyon trilogy beginning with *The Nighthawk*, (work in progress,) and in *Cold Remains*, I have deliberately kept the chapters to four, but no more than six pages long.

4. THE WHAT'S NEXT? FACTOR

Should be ever-present as you write. Keep things moving, but allow breathing spaces for descriptions and for your characters to reminisce and analyse events and others.

IGNORE THE FOLLOWING AT YOUR PERIL!

a) **Coincidences** – Do happen in real life, but use lightly in your work. Best kept small.

b) **Twins** – Have been worked to death! Avoid like the plague.

c) **Eating And Drinking**. Don't forget to feed and water your characters, even if they've been dropped in the Outback. I've found myself having written several chapters only to realise my main character hadn't touched so much as a cup of coffee for three days!

What your characters choose to eat and drink, and how they go about it, can be revealing. Such a basic activity can make even your most evil character seem human, or more grotesque.

Exercises

i) Identify what if any, coincidences might be useful/ believable in your chiller thriller.

ii) If you *had* planned to include twins, how can this tired cliché be made more interesting? By an earlier death of one of them? An untrue claim to twinhood?

A surrogate mother who gives birth to one paid-for child, while knowing another is still 'hidden' in her body.

Chapter 26

Chapter Endings

Each chapter counts in building up the intrigue and suspense that a chiller thriller needs. Their endings can either stall the story or drive it forwards, with your reader holding their breath as to what might happen next. 'Cliffhanger' is a useful cliché, and should be your mantra as you approach that last paragraph. Create a sense of unease, of danger lurking, of rising fear to make your chapter endings a diving board into the next.

Exercises

i) Study how other chiller thriller writers achieve this. Typical killer lines are -

She took off her coat and slipped her feet out of her shoes, thinking of the Rjoca waiting in the kitchen, and her favourite armchair by the fire.

Manuel yawned and rubbed his eyes. He'd had enough for one day. Bed was beckoning, and within a minute he was in it, pulling the scratchy top blanket over his head.

ii) Do you agree?
iii) If yes, re-write them, adding drama or at least a sense of foreboding.
iv) If no, then perhaps you could consider writing literary fiction. Seriously!

Examples of Good Chapter Endings

a) In Lorna Fergusson's terrific psychological, part-historical thriller, *The Chase*, set in the Dordogne, it's Spring 1944.

Werhmacht officers Ewald Sigehart and his deputy Strücker are in the Hunting Chamber of *Le Sanglier*, the house that will, some fifty years later, become Netty and Gerald Feldwick's new home. WWII isn't yet over.

Sigehart has just had sex with Mathilde, a local girl…

Then it was over. The pinned creature fell, to her knees, on the floor.

In the shadows, an echo of distant laughter, like the steel-wire plucking of a harpsichord.

Ewald came out of his daze to find her dressed and clutching the rim of her hat once more in two childlike fists, held close and high to her chest, like a squirrel holding a nut. Her voice was high, strained, but she had to know. He would let Didier go now, wouldn't he?

The door was unbolted. Mathilde was gone. He sank into a chair. Bile rose up within him. That he would have done this! Thank God no-one would know. She would not talk.

Strücker knocked all too discreetly, entered all too tactfully. Ewald quelled his hate as best he could, but barked at him all the same. Strucker in all patience replied that the man was waiting as arranged outside.

Ewald sent Strücker out, and sat alone for five minutes before going out into the whispering curiosity of the night, to negotiate with the 'mauvais Maquis'; the man who had infiltrated the local group and would betray them to him. It was always as well to have more than one way of achieving one's objective.

He would have the prisoners shot, though, as well. It had to be. Even Didier. Especially Didier. Get the job done. Get out of here. Alles in ordnung.

What I love about this short, italicised excerpt of the chapter entitled Alles in Ordnung, is how the writing's richness doesn't impede the momentum or dilute the air of menace. Similes can all too often be clichéd, but not here. A terrific ending, full of tension.

b) From *Office For the Dead*, the third thriller in my DI Martin Webb trilogy, which is still being edited. A man's corpse has been found in a container at Portsmouth docks and a nearby crane driver shot dead. He has a step-daughter in Malvern who's gone missing. Back in the Midlands, DC Martin Webb is making enquiries.

Mr. Poplinsky was almost deaf. Greedy and deaf, that much was clear. No, he'd shouted down the phone. He didn't know if his tenant in number 41, Severn Street had a lock-up. They were separate, belonging to anonymous individuals he'd never met. However, when Martin informed him of the raid, his tone changed. Yes, no problem, he'd call a friend to come and fix the lock in half an hour and would it be impertinent of him to ask if the cops would pick up the tab?

Creep, thought Martin as he returned to the house, still puzzling over those dogs' bowls and the lack of any visible dog. He also tried to fathom out where Tasha Dobbs and that carrier bag had gone. A fourteen year old with a dodgy family growing more dodgy by the minute. As he stared out of the bleary kitchen window which overlooked the weedy patch outside, he called Malvern and asked Bryn Griffiths to fix surveillance on Grove Lane till he got there to search at three o'clock.

Twenty minutes before Dora's result.

"Sure. You having a fun day?" his colleague quipped.

"You could say that."

Martin wasn't going to let on he resented him his desk by the heater. Nor give him the chance to try out some new joke. Why? Because of bricks. A block of odd looking ones set into the lock-up's wall which abutted on to the property's so-called garden. They didn't match the others at all and he wondered how the hell *that* had been missed during the so-called search.

"No more playing at jockeys, you," he said distractedly. "This is going to be big."

Dog shit everywhere. All shapes and colors. His hastily eaten bacon roll began to shift in his stomach as he picked his way over the weedy pungent grass towards the brick wall.

Don't be sidetracked, he told himself, all too aware of both the hidden tumbler and the urine sample in an empty aspirin jar pressing against his ribs under his shirt, leaving his hands free. The newer-looking bricks wobbled encouragingly in his grasp and soon, having extracted one and then the rest, he was able to crawl through the gap into the gloomy space beyond.

Jesus.

He steadied himself against the van's rear door. The shit on his boots now in competition with something else, sickly, choking, making him sneeze. Air freshener. The kind his mum had used in the Blackheath house's bathrooms. But that wasn't all. With eyes more accustomed to the darkness, he began to distinguish what seemed to be piles of rags strewn to the right-hand side of the van. But they weren't rags. Far from it. The dead eyes for a start. Six of them, trapping him like a fly in amber, so he failed to see the gun's black barrel pointing his way, nor the twitching gloved fingers poised on its trigger.

Chapter 27

To Quote Or Not To Quote?

Adding an appropriate quotation or even the origin of a word in your title, can reflect and enhance the mood of your chiller thriller. If you're considering using a quotation or two, venture off the beaten track for less well-known examples. The Oxford Book of Quotations is a good starting point, however, try casting a wider net on the internet for both quotes and poetry. It's simpler and cheaper to choose material that's out of copyright. As for searching word origins, again, a good dictionary and the internet should prove fruitful.

Exercises

i)   Research at least 5 possible quotations.

ii) Make up your own! Part of the quotation can even form your title.

Examples

a) From *Cold Remains.*
   Each heart has its graveyard, each household its dead,
   And knells ring round us wherever we tread.
   Mary T. Lathrap 'Unfinished Lines.'

b) From *Cloven.*
   I am a pilgrim here
   An alien on my way.
   Dafydd Jones, drover, from Caeo
   The night wind whispers in my ear, The moon shines in my face; A burden still of chilling fear, I find in every place.
   John Clare, from 'To Mary'

c) From *Carcass*.

Carcass - The skeleton or framework of a structure when its life or vitality has ceased. Its remains or shell. (14th century. From old French *carcasse*)

"Here pity is alive when it is dead."

Dante. 'The Divine Comedy.' (Inferno XX28)

'So when we say a man is living, it should be understood that the man has the use of his reason, which is special to him, and is the actualizing of his noblest part. And so the man who cuts himself off from reason, and has recourse only to his animal senses, does not live as a man, but as an animal.'
Convivio II. Vii 3-4
Dante. 'The Divine Comedy.'

DATES and TIMES at the start of each chapter can add pace and flavour. However, in Sarah Rayne's latest chiller, *The Silence*, the first chapter's date is 200 - . Somewhere between 2001 and 2009. This interesting device avoids having to mention precise news and events of a particular year.

Chapter headings, too, if carefully chosen. In *The Chase*, author Lorna Fergusson uses French phrases which hint at the chapters' content.

CHAPTER NUMBERS or LETTERS? XII or 12 or Twelve, or any other numerals/symbols?

You decide what best suits your material. In *The Fold*, with its mediaeval timeslip, I begin chapters with numbers in English morphing into Occitan and Latin. Again, see what other authors have done. Originality, even in this detail, can pay dividends

Chapter 28

The Pros And Cons Of Prologues

Too often Prologues are formulaic and easily forgotten. How many more hapless victims (usually young and female) do we need lying chained to a bed, or being chased through a wood, or bundled off in a strange car? These often herald a similarly unambitious novel; certainly no chiller thriller-with-a-difference.

However, a memorable Prologue can give the reader a visceral taste of exciting things to come, either by foreshadowing a future or as part of the novel's backstory. The reader will be on alert, waiting to recognise where, in the scheme of things, this nugget belongs. Usually written in the present tense, the character/s involved is/are also often nameless.

Exercise
i)   Which of the following examples of three very different prologues drew you into another world?
ii) Jot down your responses. These will help your own, should you choose to write one.
iii) If so, write your own possible Prologue. Try to keep it to one page in length. Try to convey a rising tension. Fear. Again, setting and weather can play a big part.

Examples
a) From *A Night With No Stars*, foreshadowing a terrible murder in 1987 on the Ravenstone Estate near Rhayader, mid-Wales.

PROLOGUE
It is the "no time" when the thin veils between the two worlds of the earthly year - the Samhain and the Beltane - are at their most fragile. When cosmic order is suspended and the ancient dead

rise up to stir the souls of the living.

The seven Pleiades are also rising in the north-east sky and Beltane dawns as if the first in all creation. While the sun slides upwards into the acid blue, licking away the night's sharp frost, the young inhabitants of Rhayadr-gwy wake up to the prospect of a day without school. A Baker Day of empty classrooms, silent playgrounds, yet nevertheless a day full of possibilities. When anything can happen.

For those on farms there's winter silage to cut and stock to primp and preen for tomorrow's Gamallt Show. For those without land but possessing boots and bikes, there are hills and valleys with stones glistening under laughing river water.

There's laughter too on the Ravenstone estate, but by the time the ravens have left the alders' branches to make a single rogue cloud against the blue, that laughter dies to a silence of fear. The killing room won't know the sun until late afternoon but its damp shade is the perfect home for slaughter; its dimness the only blessing for those who must watch...

Footsteps now. The drag of steel-tipped heels on stone, enough to cause sparks. The scratch of fingernails against bone as a knife's dull glow appears. Do those lads on the hills who are downing their beer or the girls undressing in the grass hear the scream which follows? Does anyone stop from their pleasures to wonder what crime has deserved such punishment? No, because the air already sings with suffering and in those ancient rural parts, familiarity has bred not compassion but contempt.

And in the aftermath, while the sun clears the high bank with its scalp of scrubby trees and the chimney's smoke dwindles and dies, one thing is certain. A reign of madness has begun.

b) From the historical thriller *Isabella's War* by Julie-Ann Corrigan, which is currently under consideration by a leading literary agent, The eponymous, main protagonist's heavily pregnant mother is about to be murdered after giving birth to her.

PROLOGUE

A farmhouse near Sabadell, 18 kilometres north of Barcelona. Spain.

November 1937.

The skinny Spanish boy turned from the broken window cutting his arm on the jagged glass. He fell backwards off the ledge and hit the ground hard. He made no sound.

He retched and wiped his mouth in one swift movement, more worried a Nationalist soldier would hear him than about the *vomito* seeping inside his shirt. Dizziness and the foul smell of his own sick threatened his balance. He took a deep breath and steadied himself; then climbed back onto the ledge and continued to peer inside.

And watched.

The girl he'd grown up with was lying prostrate on the wooden table, her legs in a perfect V; like scissors. Her stomach wide open. Blood dripped to form a neat pool on the stone floor.

Her screams made his heart hurt. 'Scilla, I'm here,' he said to her inside his head. 'Here, by the window.' He thought by using her childhood nickname, she would hear his thoughts. He rubbed the peeling paint of the window frame gently, pretending he was stroking her sweat-drenched forehead.

But it was useless.

The terrified woman, who had been cowering silently in the corner, cut the cord with a rusty knife and roughly snatched the baby from its mother's ruptured womb. He didn't know if it was alive or dead, but then it whimpered. The woman covered its face with her hand and the baby became quiet.

He looked back towards the table just long enough to see the man who had ordered the murder – because he knew this *was* murder. He studied the officer; knowing the harsh features well enough, but now etched every detail, line and furrow into his memory. Especially the eyes; eyes that held nothing inside. They were the eyes of a madman.

He heard a noise and scrambled from the ledge to hide in an outbuilding from where he watched the same woman push open the door of the farmhouse with her foot. She held the baby tight to her chest and ran down the dusty track, never looking back.

He waited and watched. Two soldiers appeared from the house, both obviously covered in Scilla's blood. They now carried her out.

An old rag was wrapped around her abdomen, holding in the contents of her gut.

He could hear her low moans. Her once vibrant and dark, lilac blue eyes were fading, but she was still alive.

Dear God, please let Scilla die soon.

They carried her down the same track. The officer sauntered behind, kicking up damp lumps of dirt to cover the wide trail of blood. Always tidy. Always careful.

He guessed they were taking her to the roadside ditches where previously, he and his mother had seen Nationalists disposing of bullet-ridden Republican bodies. But the three men carried on. She was small – carrying her was easy.

He followed behind, unseen, realising they weren't heading for the road after all; instead walking towards the hill where the neglected olive grove was, like the rest of Catalonia, slowly dying.

It was when they reached the old twisted trees – a place where he and Scilla had once played hide and seek – that he would feel true fear. He could have run away, back down the hill. It would have been the most sensible action. But he couldn't; he had to watch. It was the very least he could do. So he stayed with his fear.

And it stayed with him.

c) Prologue from David Evans' *Torment*, which foreshadows a grim future. This crime thriller is currently short-listed for the prestigious CWA Debut Dagger Award.

Monday 6th March 1989

He carried the limp, lifeless burden down the creaking wooden stairs. He'd closed the door at the top behind them and the only light came from two 40 watt bulbs in holders screwed to the floor joists. No-one came down here. He made sure of that. Outside, the wind whistled around the buildings. Exposed at the top of a rise, it always seemed to be blowing. The rain that had rattled the windows all day had finally stopped. As he got to the bottom of the steps, a train thundered its way past, rumbling through the floor. Listening closely, he knew it was on its way to the capital. Next stop Doncaster.

As he crossed the open space, a cobweb caught his face. He stumbled with his load as he wiped it away. She was lighter than the last one and he managed to hold on to her with one arm. Rounding a corner, he came to a door. Shifting the position of her body so it rested over his shoulder, he fumbled in his pocket for the key. Only he had access to it.

The lock was stiff, but it finally gave. He hadn't been in here for three years. He turned his back and pushed against the solid wooden door. The hinges groaned and the bottom screeched as small trapped stones ground against the floor. His eyes had adjusted to the dim light outside, but inside the room, there were no lights, the only illumination coming through the opened door. It took a few moments before he could make out the shape on the floor. The air smelled musty but there was no uncomfortable aroma of decaying flesh. That had long ceased.

Tears began to prick. How did it happen again? Why? They didn't have to come with him. Just because it was raining. Just because he offered them a lift, they didn't have to get in. And then when they came back here, they didn't have to make such a fuss. That's when he had to shut them up. He couldn't have them telling tales. What would folk think? They'd all think he was some sort of pervert. But he wasn't, he knew that. That's why they had to stay here. They'd be safe here.

He placed her gently down on the floor next to the other one, folding her arms over her chest and smoothing down her dress. Next, he carefully removed her sandals and white socks.

Above, the stumbling footsteps on the wooden floor startled him. He looked around and began to panic. He can't be found here. They'd be found. He slowly got back to his feet and stuffed the shoes and socks into his coat pocket. Tiptoeing out of the room, he pulled the door to as quietly as he could. He listened again. The footsteps continued overhead, doors opening and closing as if they were looking for him. He turned the key in the lock, then placed it in his trouser pocket before making his way back to the bottom of the stairs. He waited. Only when he heard the footsteps leave did he ascend and make his way out, satisfied his secrets were safe once more.

c) My Prologue to *Come and Be Killed.*

PROLOGUE

A fortnight's rain has bloated the bowels of North Hill. Filled each of its ancient crevices to capacity, spilling the glut of water past those few houses which cling to the westerly side, facing the grey smear of Welsh hills.

This overflow silvers the Tarmac encircling its girth. Turns the land below soft and spongy underfoot - quite treacherous in parts - the worst possible conditions for cycling or running. Or more importantly, grave digging. Yet the young man, sodden though he is, must satisfy his curiosity and follow where the lean female jogger first spotted from the road above, takes him. Her blue Lycra-clad body glitters like a magnet, pulling him still further away from an afternoon planned for other things. He pushes himself and his bike through ranks of giant late-flowering cow parsley whose umbelliferous heads bend low, weighted by moisture. Past hawthorn hedges where the Heritage Trail begins; where his target has suddenly vanished, leaving deep distinctive footprints which lead him to an iron shack, so old, so rusted that the slightest gust of wind will surely topple its frayed and flimsy sides.

His nostrils take in the whiff of sewage and lanolin from the creeping sheep in the fields beyond, but once he's eased the skewed door open, there's a different smell altogether.

Of meat. Raw meat. The kind which clings to every butcher's shop he's ever been in.

But this is no commercial butchers. And nobody's buying. Least of all him, for when he discovers what lies half-hidden in the gloomiest corner, it's as if he's wandered into Hell, and from now on, there will be no way out.

Chapter 29

Beginnings

In the end is the beginning? Is it best to write the start once you know the ending, or is this the time you cast off into uncharted waters? As I've already mentioned, this is your choice, but whatever it is, you're saying to your reader, "welcome to my world."

Beginnings are make or break to a book's success. Many agents and publishers confess to never reading beyond the first few paragraphs of books submitted to their slush piles. Why? Because they can tell pretty soon what works and what doesn't.

I'm no adherent of strict writing rules, however, being considerate to your reader should be paramount, and it behoves you, the writer, to bring your main character in at the start and ensure the reader's sitting tight on his/ her shoulder before others intervene. It also helps to briefly describe and qualify who this person is, so this is lodged in the reader's mind and doesn't need constant repetition. If your beginning is from this character's POV using the first person, they will still have to make themselves immediately real to the reader. A name is useful too, but you may want to withhold this until the time is right, or when this character is referred to by name.

Interestingly, in the start of Brian Moore's *The Statement*, the former Nazi's pursuer is known only as R. This device seems to work as he doesn't last long, and we're not lured into wanting to know more about him.

Delivering information in the right order is one of writing's challenges, and your line by line editing process should be an opportunity to check that every sentence fulfils this. What may seem clear to you, may not be to your reader, and without clarity, they will stumble.

I've read so many times that beginnings involving descriptions of weather are a no-no, but I beg to differ, and in Pierre Magnan's *The Murdered House*, I'm right there in the dark in a gale force wind and rain where a family's slaughter is about to take place. Cinematic is an understatement.

However, a warning! Kiss-of-death starters are the waking up in bed scene and a hand reaching out to smother the alarm clock. Yes, I'm yawning too...

Exercises

i) Identify a really different beginning to any chiller thriller you've read. Re-read it and ask yourself why was it so effective? Were you instantly drawn into another world? Did you feel impelled to keep reading?

ii) Try writing an opening paragraph engaging all the reader's senses, with you being in whoever's head is present. Use the first person POV.

iii) Convert this to the third person POV.

iv) Which felt more natural?

v) Has a flame begun to burn inside you? Did you want to keep writing? If so, then the show's on the road.

Examples

a) From *Whittlewood* by Suzanne Ruthven, where a successful London journalist arriving in rural Northamptonshire to interview a well-known occultist, is about to enter a dangerously alien world where anything can happen.

Chapter I

Only the very young are impervious to the raw sensuality of an English autumn. Also urbane, successful journalists whose only concept of 'going to the country' was a weekend at a large house in the Home Counties - or a general election. Alexander Martin viewed the countryside with unparalleled distaste. For the past three miles he had negotiated the narrow, twisting lanes in the wake of a lumbering farm vehicle, the driver seemingly unaware of his repeated attempts at overtaking. Finally, exasperated beyond all endurance, he had slammed his foot on the accelerator and risked the hidden dangers cunningly concealed beyond blind corners and tangled hedgerows.

His recently acquired *alter ego*, a normally gleaming Austin Healey 3000 was caked with mud from the damp verges and liberally splattered with cow dung from his abortive attempt at elbowing his way through a herd of bovine complacency. Already perspiring from frustration and flushed with annoyance, he realised he would have to make some attempt at restoring his equilibrium; for professional egotism would not allow him to arrive sweating and dishevelled for his appointment with, if not actually a 'secret, black and midnight hag', then someone who was rumoured to be a 20th century equivalent.

What on earth had induced him to agree to spending the weekend with a leading expert on the occult, he asked himself for the umpteenth time. Here was a woman who shunned publicity and yet was esteemed in the highest academic circles for her lectures on parapsychology; was retained by a serious national newspaper as a consultant on occult matters; and was rumoured to have been consulted by the Home Office during a particularly virulent outbreak of *quasi*-Satanism.

She was best known, however, for her highly successful occult novels that had topped the best selling list, with depressing regularity, for the past ten years. She catered for the public's thirst for matters supernatural and Charlotte Manning had subsequently become a household name. Nevertheless, she steadfastly refused to appear on the popular series of television programmes on The Unseen, The Unknowable and The Unpredictable.

People of his acquaintance who claimed to know her, stated she was at best eccentric and one even confided that she was a genuine witch. Photographs of her rarely appeared and those that were reproduced in the tabloids were extremely unflattering. On the other hand, those who had met her briefly at more private functions had been impressed by her personality and respected her privacy. Her books on the occult were well written and showed a tremendous depth of knowledge in her subject; subsequently over the years she had been hounded unmercifully by the tabloid press and various religious movements, who held her responsible for encouraging weak-minded individuals to follow the "sinister path of black magic and devil worship".

Up on the high road, overlooking the undulating landscape, Alex Martin drew to a halt. Climbing out of the vehicle and leaning against the metallic wing, he lit a cigarette and surveyed the view. Above him, where the land continued to rise, stood a large patch of woodland, a remnant of the ancient Whittlewood, where the monarchs of England had hunted for centuries. Like pagan incense rising from a sacrificial altar, the sweet smell of burning leaves hung in the air, shrouding the countryside in a delicate veil of wafting smoke.

The sun, already a low fiery orb on the hilltop, cast deep shadows around the small village that lay at the bottom of the winding descent. Another large tract of ancient oaks formed a protective arm around the houses, thinning out as the old trees approached a tributary of the local river. A fine mist clung to the water's edge, its wraith-like form held fast by the poplars, adding to the illusion of unreality despite the fact that he was only a stone's throw from the motorway and some twenty minutes' drive from the new city development in the next county.

Martin inhaled the last of his cigarette as he drew up the collar of his expensive cashmere overcoat. He was a city-bred animal, and although his eye could appreciate the subtle hue of a rustic autumn and his nostrils relish the crisp, fresh air, his ears could not come to terms with the awful silence. He was simply not attuned to the delicate symphony that hummed unceasingly amongst the tall, dried grasses of field and hedgerow. The cry of a bird, which was unrecognisable to him, broke his reverie and with a sigh of resignation he climbed back into the car to continue his journey.

b) My own *Malediction* opens in a small town in N.E. France, with Colette, anxious for the safety of her student son, setting off for Paris to find him. In writing this, I wanted to suggest the problem of anti-Semitism still lurking in that depressed part of N.E France. To set Colette off on her doomed journey.

I.

Thursday 21st August 1997

Colette Bataille could hear the kids down below in the Rue St. Léger on their way to the new roller-skating rink. Snatches of taunts and chants were scarred by the run of blades on tarmac and the sudden staccato jumps on and off the kerb. "Hades must be like this," she muttered, reviving her lips with a new lipstick, and enlarging both eyes with a soft crayon. Eyes that in two hours time she'd use to search her lover's face for any trace of his old longing. Father Jean-Baptiste - Robert Vidal - priest and assistant choirmaster of the Église de la Sainte Vièrge at Lanvière, who'd been put away for three weeks at the Villerscourt Boot Camp for reasons never fully explained.

There'd been whispers, of course - the most consistent being that his driving ambition with his young church choir here in Lanvière, had spilled over into obsession. That he'd worked them too hard, too long and issued threats to those who'd been absent. But who had dared betray him?

Lips had stayed sealed.

She rinsed her hands then checked her watch before peering round her son Bertrand's bedroom door, as though this would somehow return him to his refuge. She then left the apartment. Twenty steps of black marble down into the catacomb of post-war design, before the sudden slab of sunlight. She squinted up to her windows - saw the red pelargoniums drifted against the down pipe, and her neighbour Dolina Levy's withered eyes unmoving. Colette waved, too briefly she knew. But not briefly enough. No time to listen yet again to tales of her life in Cracow; of her husband and sister taken at gun-point and her flight into the Vosges disguised as a Red Cross nurse. She was late.

"Another sheep for Le Pape?" Growled the old woman.

"Safety in numbers." Colette's voice was thin and unconvincing. Besides, the Peugeot was boiling and she needed to find its key.

"No safety for us. Never was."

"I know and I'm sorry. Everyone is."

"Not everyone, and you'd better believe it. Just listen to them out there. And they're still children."

"It's shocking, I know."

The widow craned over her tiny balcony. Two fur slippers poked through the railings next to her cat, 'Mitzvah', corpse-like in the sun.

"Got to go, really." Colette stored the bags in the boot. His and hers and a decent picnic, then covered them over with Bertrand's old baby blanket. "Look, I'll call in when I'm back. That's a promise." She waved again, but her neighbour's face stayed grimly fearful in her mirror as she turned out into the square.

Her radio, always tuned to France Musique, was offering a preview of a newly -commissioned work for the Feast of Saint Bartholomew. Atonal chords over a pulsing drum filled her small space. Hardly saintly for the tanner, or the poor Huguenots, she thought on the roundabout for the The Forêt de Dieulet, but then *she* wasn't feeling particularly saintly either.

Ten past nine. He'd taught her that. Always to keep a note of the time. Whatever. Wherever. She smiled. Three weeks had been a long time without him, and she'd allowed work to take up her evenings, staying late at the office, staring at his church through its blinds imagining him without her. So there was no guilt when she'd asked her boss for two days off to attend the Pope's Mass at Longchamp - he'd even said the break would do her good.

Now the sun was high enough over the trees to heat her face, and she saw skin forty-four years-old. Not tanned exactly, but the way Robert had always liked it. And a curve of hair gold as the corn of Limousin, he'd once said, newly shaped for the occasion.

Her heel touched the floor. There was no other traffic, for this was a weekend route to the deer parks and the walks near Nazairolles. She thought of the modest hotel in Paris she'd booked. Just for the two of them, and her hands trembled as the road ahead melted into the haze between trees where a horse and rider cantered along the dark edge of pines.

She saw the sign for Pouilly, their agreed rendezvous, and suddenly she slowed up. Something was wrong. Two men when there should have been one, black against black like crows and Robert's hand raised as though she was a taxi. Feeling cheated, Colette found a lay-by and swung round to meet them head on.

The Dominicans were running.

c) The first of David Evans' gritty crime thrillers, *Trophies* opens in Wakefield Police Station. Here, the author sets the scene vividly and economically. I love how he moves from the general to the particular. From the town itself, to the inside of a lunch box. Memorable.

I.

Tuesday, January 24th 2000.

Wakefield; home of Double-Two shirts, Trinity Rugby League, two railway stations and a cathedral. A city with strong connections to crime; home of the highest grade prison on mainland Britain as well as West Yorkshire's Police Training College. The cathedral was once the haunt of a choirboy by the name of John

George Haigh, who gained notoriety in the late nineteen-forties as the Acid Bath murderer. Behind the cathedral and opposite the Town Hall stands Wood Street police station, a four storey stone building, battered by the wind and rain of another bleak January day.

In his first floor office, Detective Inspector Colin Fear stared into his empty sandwich box. Half past twelve and he'd finished the contents an hour ago.

d) From *Isabella's War* by Julie-Ann Corrigan, in which the eponymous Isabella begins a quest to find who, during Franco's tyranny, murdered her mother who'd just given birth to her.

I.

Paris, France.

May 1968.

Isabella.

The Chief of Police of Guipuzcoa had died, so I heard, with a look of utter surprise scratched onto his wide, waxen face. Basque patriots would whisper, then after Franco's demise talk openly about the man who had terrorised the region for years. A man who in death displayed the cowardice he had always managed to hide whilst living. As his life ebbed away, he begged his Catholic God for forgiveness. Forgiveness for murders he committed with an appalling enjoyment. Meliton Menzanas's name wasn't important, but he represented a dictatorship that had destroyed his country, and its people.

Madame Cauchon knocked on my door soon after I returned from a long walk in the *Champs-Elysées* gardens.

'Mademoiselle, this arrived while you were out.'

I looked down at my small, spindly neighbour, 'Thank you. Sorry you were bothered on a Saturday.'

'Oh, don't you worry. Always up with the larks.' She peered

at the brown envelope, 'Hope not bad news...'

I slipped it my pocket, 'Probably to do with work ... you know how it is.'

Deflated, she turned knowing I wouldn't open it now, *'Bonne journée à vous*, Mademoiselle Adami.'

She shuffled down the corridor to her own apartment. We'd lived next door to each other for seven years; I wondered how long it would be before she called me Isabella.

I slit open the telegram and, seeing the name of *Le Canard Enchainé's* editor, I threw it to one side. Satirical journalism wasn't my niche, something Babineaux knew. I'd worked for him, freelance, when he'd edited an underground socialist newspaper in Spain. He had fled Spain for his native France five years' previously; Franco's iron grip on the media had made his position, and his newspaper obsolete.

More than anyone, Babineaux was aware of my socialist leanings and empathy for the Basque fight for independence. He knew my mother had been involved in that cause during the Civil War. And that was surely why he'd sent this telegram. I re-read the flimsy piece of paper again with curiosity.

Meliton Menzanas's name had caught my eye.

Another virulent bully in a still-tortured Spain.

I knew, as did most well-informed editors around Europe, that his death opened the door to a Basque nationalist feeling that resonated well beyond the region's borders. The repercussions would become politically important. It was a story that would be far too contentious for *Le Canard*.

And so my interest was ignited as Babineaux, cleverly, had guessed.

He still had links in Spain, notably within the cauldron of the Basque region. One of these organizations had asked this legendary editor to find a freelance, left-wing and Spanish journalist to cover the Menzanas murder and report on the still fledgling Basque nationalist group ETA, who had admitted responsibility to the killing. Babineaux said he'd thought of me immediately.

The subject was too interesting to turn down.

Exercise

Having read these four quite different examples of beginnings, try analysing whether or not they drew you in. Whether you wanted to keep reading. If yes, why? If not, why?

Chapter 30

Tenses

Plain and simple or ring the changes?

The present tense is commonly used for Prologues and increasingly, throughout the novels themselves. This can lend an immediacy to your narrative, but in less confident hands, can seem clunky and forced. I'm noticing a growing trend amongst new graduates/post-graduates of creative writing degrees, to use the present tense combined with the first person POV. If you want to join this trend, that's your decision, but for the beginner writer, I'd suggest you keep to the 3rd person limited POV, and the past tense until you feel confident enough to try other alternatives. Some writers vary their tenses according to which character is featured in particular chapters. This adds variety, but demands more of the reader. Take care to be consistent. Also, to avoid lengthy backstory sections written in the pluperfect tense. These can slow up the pace, even grind it to a halt! Keep the story in real time as much as you can.

Again, look at successful, recently-published chiller thrillers and judge for yourself. I've never written anything in the future tense, but it could be exciting.

Exercises

i)   Write a paragraph using the 3rd person past tense involving your main character getting dressed.

ii)   Take this same paragraph and use the present tense.

iii)   Now use the 1st person + present tense.

iv)   Which felt the most natural to write?

Example

a) From chapter 2 of my work in progress thriller, *The Nighthawk*, set near the eastern Pyrenees. Here, the mysterious recluse, Karen Fürst is about to have her life yet again turned upside down. This first example is in the original present tense, which my agent suggested I change to the past. Line 6 proved the most tricky in both versions.

2.

Why not be like a dolphin and just stop breathing? I often ask myself. It would be so easy, so peaceful. Then, as little Liesbetje all over again, I'd see Vader and my older brothers all happily perched upon a white cloud welcoming me into their new world. Telling me there never was a mystery about their disappearance. That my over-developed imagination and above all, the sin of delusion, had wasted too much of my life.

Oh yes, I could do it tonight in bed, by pulling the annoying oxygen tubes from my nostrils and letting my lungs have their first big break since I fell from my horse. No-one would be blamed, least of all Herman, my ferociously devoted nurse whom I'd brought over from Rotterdam. Who'd helped make this half-life at least worth living...

Suddenly, I hear steel doors slamming shut, followed by footsteps thudding on the tiles outside my room. But where was he? He should be here, securing my door. Guarding me.

What on earth?

I can only turn my head to the right as I force my wheelchair round, scorching my palms on its hard, rubber wheels until I myself slide the door's first bolt across, then the next. My pulse banging in my brain...

"Dr. Fürst?"

"Who's there?"

"Martine. I was being followed through the Gorges de Salerne. Managed to lose them by the church..."

"Them?"

"Two young guys in a Silver Merc with an Aude plate. Both

wearing shades."

"Are our gates locked?"

Silence.

My voice moves up an octave. "Are our gates locked?"

b) Past tense.

2.

Why not be like a dolphin and just stop breathing? I often asked myself. It would be so easy, so peaceful. Then, as little Liesbetje all over again, I'd see Vader and my older brothers all happily perched upon a white cloud welcoming me into their new world. Telling me there never was a mystery about their disappearance. That my over-developed imagination and above all, the sin of delusion, had wasted too much of my life.

Oh yes, I could have done it last night in bed, by pulling the annoying oxygen tubes from my nostrils and letting my lungs have their first big break since I fell from my horse. No-one would be blamed, least of all Herman, my ferociously devoted nurse whom I'd brought over from Rotterdam. Who'd helped make this half-life at least worth living...

Suddenly, I heard steel doors slamming shut, followed by footsteps thudding on the tiles outside my room. But where was he? He should be here, securing my door. Guarding me.

What on earth?

I could only turn my head to the right as I forced my wheel-chair round, scorching my palms on its hard, rubber wheels until I myself slid the door's first bolt across, then the next. My pulse banging in my brain...

"Dr. Fürst?"

"Who's there?"

"Martine. I was being followed through the Gorges de Salerne. Managed to lose them by the church..."

"Them?"

"Two young guys in a Silver Merc with an Aude plate. Both wearing shades."

"Are our gates locked?"

Silence.

My voice moved up an octave. "Are our gates locked?"

Exercise

i) Which tense do *you* prefer? Why?

ii) Try changing the tenses on what *you've* done so far. Remember, you can't force things, and what feels more natural to you, will read and sound far better.

Chapter 31

Let's Get Talking

How to craft not copy dialogue.

Harold Pinter was a great exponent of what he called 'defensive dialogue' where his characters divulge little to each other, being too busy fighting their own corners. This is an interesting idea to use sparingly. Your dialogue should keep the story moving, with each character sounding different/showing different speech rhythms from the others. No reader wants to trawl through a conversation that dribbles along. Yes, in everyday life we do ramble, but on the page, this is a different kind of killer.

Characters will reveal their true selves under stress, so the more conflict and tension you create the better. In David Pinnock's frightening chiller, *Ritual,* its main protagonist, David Hanlin upon challenging the Reverend White's strange behaviour near a young girl's grave, observed how everyone in the village always laughed before they lied. This is a gem.

Some people try to 'bury' their pasts by speaking in a different way. Elocution lessons still thrive for those wanting to lose their accents for whatever reason, but maybe not all traces are lost. People shouting often revert to their true tongue, and many actors turned novelists including Linda Regan, have an acute ear for individual voices. Younger people in 'developed' countries who've been brought up with texting, will have quite different sentence structures and words from say, a seventy year-old retired civil servant. This contrast can be exciting and I believe if not overdone, these slightly different words can add interest to the mix. My very (rightly) picky editor at Pan Macmillan was quite happy with the local Lilith Leakes' dialect in *Wringland.*

With historical thrillers, (even 10 years ago is classed as

'historical,') the danger is to choke the reader with a form of English that's impossible to wade through. Wear the rhythms and wordage of your chosen times lightly. Distillation not strangulation!

Exercises

i) Investigate 3 different dialects in the UK. Many still survive.

ii) If your work is set wholly, even partly elsewhere, try the same research. Every region has its linguistic differences.

iii) If your work is historical or includes an historical strand, check the language of the time, and also read how another historical thriller writer using that era, handles speech and POVs.

iv) Listen to radio plays where each voice counts. (Audio tapes of books that use just one narrator aren't quite as useful.)

v) Create your own bare dialogue of at least 10 lines between your main character and one other, with no 'frills.' No 'he said/she said' etc. No background detail. It should reflect a moment of conflict. Both speakers should 'sound' different.

vi) Create a dialogue of at least 16 lines between any three characters, using 'he said/she said,' etc and including information of the surroundings. During this, something important should be revealed. This may of course, be conveyed by one of the characters' POV.

Examples

a) In *Runt* by Niall Griffiths, the Welsh teenage narrator, has his own version of English. His step-father is 'NoTDad' and his dog is called Arrn after the sound of its bark. There's hardly any punctuation yet the story, which is full of emotion, rattles along.

b) In *On Writing,* Stephen King sees no need for 'whispered,' 'shouted' etc. Instead, just use 'said.' Interesting to try, but over 300+ pages, it's a big ask!

c) Here are two pieces of 'bare' dialogue. The first, from my *Malediction,* in which Dominique Mathieu, reluctant recruit, is quizzing Robert Vidal about Colette's missing student son.

Mathieu fell silent, then when he'd recovered, tried a different tack.

"What's he like?"

"OK. I suppose. Trouble was though, she kept trying to push him on to me. Said he needed a role model, a father figure, for God's sake. She wanted him in the choir. That was her thing. Every Saturday she'd send him over to me with a begging letter."

"A maman's love no less."

"I told her she was more like a Jewish mother. She didn't like that at all. Just kept saying it would do him good, build up his confidence. But that's something he was never short of. Cocky little shit if you must know. He could never leave it alone."

"What exactly?"

"The fact we were seeing each other. He used to hang around the flat, always bloody there like mould on a cheese - once when we thought he was out, he was hiding. Actually caught us at it..."

"Oh Lord."

"Can't prove it, but I think he let old Toussirot know."

"The Bishop of Ramonville?"

"Correct. And the rest is history, including Villerscourt."

Spasms of shouting from one of the encampments ended the brief silence.

"He must be about my age."

"Near enough but old enough to know better." Vidal's face had changed. He'd said too much already and Mathieu knew it.

d) From the taut, psychological thriller, *Falling Suns*, by Julie-Ann Corrigan, in which Jonathan, the journalist, has called on Rachel, whose young son Joe is missing. There's a great description of her mother too, with a deliberate repetition on line 6 up.

Jonathan pulled his jacket tighter around his body, and raked a hand through thick, wavy black hair. His soft brown eyes rippled with thought. Expressive, innately kind and enquiring eyes.

'Do you want to talk?' he said, relaxed knowing Liam was absent.

'About Joe?'

'I've come to see you as a friend.'

'I know, Jonathan.'

'You're looking terrible.'

'I know that too.'

'Are you and Liam okay?'

'No, not really.'

'Does Gillespie have any real leads?'

'No, not really.'

'You shouldn't be here, alone. What about your family … your mother, your dad?'

I laughed at that one. My mother, my dad had told me, as gently as he could, wasn't coping very well. She wasn't coping very well walled up in her pristinely clean semi-detached bungalow. I could see her, sitting upright in the armchair. Hair coiffured and backcombed. Lipstick perfectly pencilled onto thinning lips. One of her regulation white and plain blouses buttoned high towards her aging, lined neck. Not worrying about me, or indeed her grandson, but about how all this would affect her standing in a community that she shunned as not being good enough for her.

e) Dialogue with actions, from my *Wringland* where Abbie Parker has met old Lilith Leakes who reveals a significant piece of information. As I've already mentioned, my editor felt the old woman's dialect didn't impede the reading process. What do you think?

"Make a wish," said the crone.

Abbie tried to pull back.

"Ya mother says."

"Leave her alone. She's dead!"

"Now!"

And Abbie's grief and battered dreams flowed like the neap tide that heaps and spreads itself, flooding and drowning the waiting land.

"Tha's better." Lilith Leakes smiled in a black line, as the cadaver rejoined the others. "But tha's not the end of it. There's the history."

"My history?" Abbie wiped her eyes with her cuff.

"No, Black Fen. The worst of all." She scooped her grey grass hair back into a rough knot, changing her face into little more than a skull. "Ya got a few moments?"

Out of habit, Abbie checked her watch.

"I'm late already."

"Ya need to know, but better make it soon. Afore I'm taken off in a bag."

The urgency took Abbie aback. "What about Wednesday?"

"Soon enough." The hermit wrapped her filthy coat around her and gathered up her salvage. "Evenings is best. I'm settled in by then. Ya know where I live?"

"Yes. Just past the Whiplash. Mrs. Clapman told me."

Lilith Leakes gave a dismissive shrug. "Never 'eard of her. Still, I don't doubt some folks round here know more about me than I do mesen. Now, I do find tha' diverting."

Abbie was aware of the seconds eroding further into the afternoon, but she still had questions to ask.

"Do you know a Rosie Quinn by any chance?"

The other woman stopped and stared so hard that Abbie had to look away.

"Please, it's very important."

"I do and I don't." She finally closed up the bag. "Why ya asking?"

"She needs help."

"My need's greater than hers."

"But you gave her some old dolls. Why?"

The old woman sucked in her cheeks and spat out a bolus of phlegm.

"I'll tell ya when I sees ya next. And the rest. I'm weary now."

Abbie took a calculated risk. "Will that include Martha Robinson?"

The old woman jabbed a blood-smeared finger at her sleeve.

"I never talk o' the Devil away from my hearth, nor should ya, if ya'n got a whit o' sense."

Then Lilith Leakes, spinster of the parish and last in the line of land reclaimers, walked away, bent low against the clearing sky, while her new acquaintance watched till she'd disappeared.

Pulling her suit jacket tight about her, Abbie wondered if the faint sound coming in from the sea was from scavenging birds or the beginnings of that same terrible laughter.

Chapter 32

Mind Your Language

The words to use.

The leaves on the plane tree next to the Hôtel de Ville shivered to the ground.

Or, the leaves on the tree next to the Hôtel de Ville fell to the ground.

Which version creates more of a mood? Why?

You don't necessarily have to write the pared-down prose of Elmore Leonard or Raymond Chandler, brilliant though it is, to be a good thriller writer. Read widely within the genre and you'll soon find a kindred spirit whose work will reinforce how *you* want to deliver your story. To make your characters live and breathe; build increasing suspense and conflict. And the more you write, the more your voice will truly be your own. This is thrilling in itself.

Try varying the lengths of your sentences. Feel the flow and rhythm of your words. Writing free verse poetry can help achieve the necessary *inner* rhythms of readable prose. I can usually tell which prose writers are also poets. Their work seems to possess a natural fluency.

If, for example, your chiller thriller is being told through the POV of say, a young, Catholic woman living in Milan and a man originally from Boston USA, their connections to these places will probably show. He may use words such as 'faucet' instead of 'tap.' She may use references to saints etc. in her inner thoughts. You have to *be* them. In their heads, walking in their shoes...

Continual swearing and blaspheming can weary the reader. I was also advised not to use the 'c' word, but have seen it often enough. Remember that the views on living people, race and religion that your characters express, cannot be attributed to you.

However, we sadly don't live in an age of tolerance, so be wary.

Let your Thesaurus and dictionary be your constant companions and be well-used by the time you've reached the end of your book.

'Padding' words including 'of,' 'that' and 'because' can litter and slow up your story. Also check how many 'it/its/it's have crept into your manuscript. Repetitions too, unless deliberately there for emphasis.

Avoid beginning a new line or paragraph with e.g.; 'Having bought a bagel,...' Or, 'Kicking the car door shut, she went over to...'

Begin sentences with an active verb to create more immediacy. For example;

a) He bought a bagel...'

b) She kicked the car door shut and went over to...'

Exercises

i) Your main protagonist is looking for a particular place/house/other. Use whichever tense and viewpoint feels most natural and ties in with what you've written so far. Also include a telling detail. E.g., a piece of litter. A particular smell...

ii) Read your previous day's work through line by line before moving on. Are there unintended clichés? (Remember, certain characters and even an authorial viewpoint will use them.) Is there lazy writing with too much of the aforementioned 'padding?' Can you make some verbs and adjectives more vivid? Reading out loud may cover a multitude of sins, but it can be useful for spotting repetitions.

iii) Former and latter are designed to confuse your reader. If they have to refer back to something, you could lose them.

iv) Would you agree the following is lazy writing? If so, identify why, and re-write.

It was dark and cold and the street and its street lamps didn't show up much which didn't help Josh locate number 8 where the stripper would have started without him.

Example

a) From chapter 4 in my *Cloven*, where the fourteen year-old mute and crippled Siân Richards is getting ready to leave home and her hostile mother. (I later wondered if the Welsh language 'lilt' might have subliminally influenced the rhythm in those chapters written from her viewpoint. Or not.)

'Eat up, girl. Your brother'll be here soon.'

Siân stared at the slab of bread whose burnt oats stood up from its surface like rabbit droppings. Then her head slumped, suddenly full of the sleep her recent nightmare had stolen. Her nose hit the table hard.

A slap stung her ears. The fourteen-year-old tried to stand as, in protest, her mother snatched the crust and crammed it into her own mouth. 'A lodger you are to be sure, Siân Richards, and in my book never to be anything else.'

Her daughter watched crumbs fall from those tight dry lips that had not uttered one word of affection to her either before or after her accident. Gazed at those washed-out eyes, like the pools in the lane. Not like those of her father, Geraint Richards, which were deep and dark. But what was the use thinking that? What use was anything? He wouldn't be back from his job as a caster with the Dowlais ironworks till summer at least, and she missed him more than her old life itself. 'Dribbling again, are you?' The woman rubbed Siân's chin with her apron. 'The Lord knows how I try. The Lord knows.'

Then Siân suddenly froze.

Her brother had arrived – and something was going on. It was as if his shadow reached her from the door, bringing in a draught of icy air. Next came his voice, so like their father's she could pretend it was him, but for the smell. Her brother's boots were green with dung and his clothes reeked like ox skin.

'She'll need a coat, Mam.' Tomos went over to the range and plucked a trotter from the cold broth. He let the greasy stock drip down his front as he sucked, then returned the trotter to the pot. His mother, Mair Richards, watched from the stairs as if he were a stranger. Two years away from the Plas Newydd hearth and having his own herds had changed him. He licked his lips with a huge red tongue as Siân listened to her mother's silence, except for her opening and shutting of cupboard doors.

'Why a coat? For me? He's never bothered before whether I freeze or burn.'

The request had also thrown Mair Richards into confusion, and the girl wondered what her mother could possibly find for her. She saw Tomos open the small cupboard set below the room's one main beam and unearth a sliver of cheese edged with mould. He dropped it to the floor and trod it into a mess. Then he sniffed.

'Something's pissed itself in here, and I'm telling you straight, it's not me.'

He bent down and lifted the hem of Siân's skirt. 'Hey, I'm not putting up with her stinking like the drains.'

'You'll have to. I'm finished with her.' The forty-eight year old woman held up her husband's coat: the best *brethyn cartref*, patched and mended, still creased from lying in the honeymoon chest. 'You don't deserve it, mind.' Her mother laid it over Siân's back. It felt the warmest thing in that miserable hovel and for a moment their eyes met. Eyes looking from as far apart as other worlds yet, for a moment, Siân imagined a tiny smile stretched her mother's lips.

'Now you're to make no bother for your brother, since he's

good enough to take you.'

'*Take me where? Where am I going?*' The girl's face searched from one to the other.

'You tell her.'

'No.'

Chapter 33

Fight The Lazy Flab

How to avoid a sagging middle.

It's easy to get carried away by your fingertips on the keyboard or wrapped around your pen, but the middle of a thriller can, like our own, show signs of over-indulgence. Who hasn't, while reading another author's work, skipped several chapters in the hope of finding that momentum they were enjoying earlier? It may be because those chapters have grown longer than at the start, or the 'what next?' factor has deserted them, and you find yourself skimming page after page that details a tedious meeting or uneventful journey.

A thriller or any other genre fiction shouldn't be akin to a hurdle race where all obstacles are of a similar, modest height and distance apart. Think of it more as the Grand National steeplechase over varied fences, some quite frankly dangerous and others less so by comparison, where the course itself is unique for its perilous bends and unique length.

Moving towards your eventual climax and ending, it will pay you to re-assess your first 40,000 words and re-discover the earlier dynamism. I find it helpful to stop writing at this point, print out these pages and read through them with a pen handy to arrow onwards any possible 'threads' even a sub-plot or two that might have died or could be created.

Then, including these, try and draft a fresh diagram for your story's progress.

For example; Is the mysterious teenager who seemed to be following your main protagonist on his/her way to the bank on page 30, still be around on page 50? If so, and if he or she could become significant enough, perhaps you can give them their own POV, until the situation between the two is developed and resolved during the rest of the book.

Think of your story as a tapestry, with these 'threads' – some inevitably more promising than others – woven in and out from beginning to end, so that any potential 'sagging middle' will be supported and carried through.

Also check that each chapter ending carries the suspense onwards. Nowhere is this device more vital than in the middle.

A surprise letter, phone call or discovery can re-ignite the momentum. For example, in Johan Theorin's *The Darkest Room*, when Joakim Westin's missing wife's body is finally discovered below the jetty at Eel Point. This moves him to re-visit their earlier life in Stockholm.

In Steig Larssen's last of his trilogy, *The Girl Who Kicked the Hornet's Nest*, Lisbeth Salander is in hospital secretly making contact with her computer hacker friends to find further evidence to back her case for freedom. In a lesser writer's hands, this could have been a self-indulgent interlude where she's just thinking about her past and dreams for the future. Instead, there's action and tension and a rising sense of danger. For some time, I did wonder about her 'helpful' doctor. Whether he could be trusted. And this again, shows Larssen's skill at sowing doubt in the reader's mind.

Exercise

i) See if this sagging problem exists in the current thriller you are reading.

ii) If you belong to a writers' group or other writing community, or online, raise this question and find out what others have experienced. It's another silent killer.

Examples

a) Half way through *Dark Harvest*, DI Martin Webb discovers the eviscerated body of investor and retiree, Richard Greener in a reservoir in the Malvern Hills. This gives the thriller's engine a surge which propels it towards the even grimmer climax.

Martin listened hard to the night and checked his watch. 3 a.m. Sleep's deepest time and burglars' friend The water made seductive little lapping noises as its ripples hit the boulders shoring up its southernmost end. His torch beam brought the various warning signs into alarming focus. No diving, bathing or fishing.

As if...

Just as he was about to retrace his steps up the black hill, something odd caught his eye, wedged up against the huge rocks. No, it definitely wasn't litter. Too big for a start, but driftwood? Abandoned clothing? He couldn't quite tell. As he slithered closer, he soon realized he was staring at the fully-clothed body of a late middle-aged man, lying face up on the water, whose grey-haired head butted repeatedly against the unyielding granite.

Richard Greener had probably not been there longer than two hours...

Death had replaced that Boxing Day smile with a bloated grimace and blind, screwed-up eyes. But there was more. Closer inspection showed a clean, gaping wound extending like some giant fish's operculum from ear to ear under the dead man's chin, and as far as he could tell, this was the only visible wound. Had the man bled to death before or after entering the water? He wondered. And why here, in a spot where in daylight at least, privacy would be impossible?

Martin then recalled that letter he'd nicked from Anchors Away. Had selling those shares been a prelude to suicide? Had Caritas that seemed a thriving blue-chip company, proved too much of a problem for their investor? Or had he been murdered?

He peered again at the man's dark overcoat, then realized the obvious. That in fresh water such as this, only the very lightest of objects might float for a while before succumbing. Never mind a fully-grown adult.

Instinct told him to pull him out and perhaps hide him until he'd got help. Reason disagreed.

0.3.44 a.m.

What the hell could he do without a functioning phone? If he left the body here, someone else might take the law into their own hands. Even an animal predator. Just as he tried dialing again, a violent, artificial light suddenly appeared from his left. The beam focused on to him, so fixed, so blinding, that the phone slipped from his grasp and bounced towards the water.

Plop.

The most ominous sound in the world. So, who the fuck was tracking him? Who'd known he'd come here? And yet another unwelcome thought - could he be next? A heavy blow to the side of his head, knocked him back into the water.

b) From halfway in *Spider Light* by Sarah Rayne, where Godfrey Toy of Quire House is about to make a discovery which keeps the suspense and momentum moving.

He made himself grip the torch more firmly and the eerie illusion vanished, and Godfrey remembered that light and shadows were notorious for twisting quite ordinary things into something sinister-looking. Still, he would reassure himself before he went away.

Still gripping the torch, he went forward. The floor sagged as he walked across it, and the worn joists creaked like giant's bones, and the nearer he got to the rotting tank the more it looked as if human hair really was spilling out through the rotting wood, and as if a human hand really was reaching out... And the beating of the horrible clock no longer sounded like the minutes ticking away, it really did sound like a human heart.

The hellish tattoo of a terrified human heart in the minutes before death...?

Oh for pity's sake! He was standing in the middle of a mediaeval water mill with a smeary twilight all round him and Twygrist's hideous clock pounding the seconds away, and all he could do was quote Edgar Allen Poe! He reached the water-wheel in its decaying tank, and taking a deep breath, shone the light.

And oh God, it really was a human hand that was reaching out through the rotted wood, and it really was human hair that was spilling out. Godfrey felt as if his temperature had soared to at least a hundred, but an icy hand seemed to be clutching at the base of his stomach. There *was* somebody inside that grim tank. Somebody had fallen inside it – all the way down – and was lying under the monstrous teeth of the waterwheel. And the force of the fall had caused the decaying wood to rupture so that whoever it was had half fallen through.

Amy? Please don't let it be Amy. But if it does have to be Amy – and I know it won't be – please let her be just injured, nothing worse than that. A bit bruised – a broken arm or leg. Repairable. And let her just be knocked out, because you come round from being knocked out...

Godfrey began to shake so violently that he thought he might fall down, but he took several deep breaths, and then set the torch on the ground so that it created a little pool of light against the water tank. It showed up the burst-open sides, and the little pool of black brackish water that had spilled out, and it showed up the reaching hand, glinting on a square-set amber ring in an old-fashioned setting. Godfrey recognised the ring at once: Amy always wore it; she liked Victorian jewellery. He knelt down and reached for the hand.

Dreadful. Oh God, it was the most dreadful thing he had ever known. The nails were broken and bloodied, and the hand itself was appallingly bruised and torn. But the skin was cold and flaccid, and it was Amy, just as he had known it was, and she was quite certainly dead. Oliver's bright lovely wife was dead...

Chapter 34

Who's Doing What?

And let's also be clear who's speaking.

If your reader has to pause to wonder what on earth is going on and who on earth is speaking, you've lost them. They won't trust you again. Show them some consideration!

It's easy with TV, film (even with subtitles) and plays; not quite so with radio and audio tapes, but writers of books have the hardest task of all, making everything real on the page. My wonderful editor at Pan Macmillan used to say, 'spell it out. You can always cut back on the pedantry later.' Name overload is just as much a problem as not enough. It's annoying to constantly see someone's name when we know it's them speaking. Balance is the secret.

You should indent a tab each time a new character speaks. Where a character's speech is interrupted by a section of prose, that speech continues on the same line. You should also indent a tab whenever a new action happens.

Without the correct punctuation, your work can be seriously undermined, so give this priority. The semi-colon is useful where a comma is too weak and a full stop is too strong. Here are two little comma gems to add sense to the following...

The taxi nudged the kerb near his feet and, without warning, its driver tumbled out onto the road.

Exercises

i) Have you been confused while reading a particular book? Why? Write down any specific examples, noting layout and punctuation, or lack of. This specific analysis should help you enormously.

ii) Re-visit your own writing and in a detached way, check

you are certain who's doing and saying what. You'll be surprised how many ambiguities there are.

iii) Try correcting the errors in the excerpt below. Then look at the correct version underneath. Did you find them all?

Line 10 of the correct example is useful in that Rita is still speaking after her question in line 3. However, because line 9 is indented, her continuing speech is put on the next line, and left justified.

Examples

a) From Book 1, chapter 1 of *Overspill* where Rita and Frank Martin are taking their two kids on a short seaside break. The trip is doomed from the start.

Rita glanced at her husband as they joined the M45, her wipers on full, as the sky had turned black and traffic was little more than a blur. "You OK?" He still seemed in pain. Unable to make that right foot comfortable at all, and yet at odd times, when perhaps he'd not seen her looking, he'd walked on it normally, just like his old self. Then the traitorous thought had occurred to her - what if this so-called "injury" was all a con? That something else was cooking? And, knowing him of old, no way would he ever let on to her. He nodded, his lips drawn together. His frown deepening. "Maybe the sea water'll do it good." She suggested. "Ease the joint a bit."

"For fuck's sake, woman, I'm not some bloody race-horse."

"Dad saying bad words." Kayleigh gloated from the back. She leant forwards and gave his shoulder a playful smack.

"Well, you'll have to do something," she added. "You'll need to be driving again, that's for sure." She refrained from saying "or we'll have to get re-housed with the Council. Or we lose every-thing." Not with the kids listening. Not today. In fact, she didn't even want to *think* about leaving their neat rented semi in Briar

Bank, with its cared-for garden, all its memories. Didn't want to think his boss might be just spinning him along.

"Hey, will there be driftwood where we're goin'?" Jez asked suddenly, opening his farmyard box and fingering the plastic hens and sheepdogs lying on their sides. His art teacher at the Primary School had brought in two carvings she'd made after a trip up north to Bamburgh Castle. A horse's head and something that looked like an old man, all bent over. He loved their strange, smooth forms and had talked of nothing else for days.

"I doubt it son." He winced as he tried to turn round. "Folks don't leave bits o' wood lyin' around for long these days. Anyhow, why you askin'?"

b) Rita glanced at her husband as they joined the M45, her wipers on full, as the sky had turned black and traffic was little more than a blur.

"You OK?"

Frank still seemed in pain. Unable to make that right foot comfortable at all, and yet at odd times, when perhaps he'd not seen her looking, he'd walked on it normally, just like his old self. Then the traitorous thought had occurred to her - what if this so-called "injury" was all a con? That something else was cooking? And, knowing him of old, no way would he ever let on to her.

He nodded, his lips drawn together. His frown deepening.

"Maybe the sea water'll do it good," she suggested. "Ease the joint a bit."

"For fuck's sake, woman, I'm not some bloody race-horse."

"Dad saying bad words." Kayleigh gloated from the back. She leant forwards and gave his shoulder a playful smack.

"Well, you'll have to do something, Frank," Rita added. "You'll need to be driving again, that's for sure." She refrained from saying, "or we'll have to get re-housed with the Council. Or we lose everything." Not with the kids listening. Not today. In fact, she didn't even want to *think* about leaving their neat rented semi in Briar Bank, with its cared-for garden, all its memories. Didn't want to think his boss might be just spinning him along.

"Hey, will there be driftwood where we're goin'?" Jez asked suddenly, opening his farmyard box and fingering the plastic hens and sheepdogs lying on their sides. His art teacher at the Primary School had brought in two carvings she'd made after a trip up north to Bamburgh Castle. A horse's head and something that looked like an old man, all bent over. He loved their strange, smooth forms, and had talked of nothing else for days.

"I doubt it, son." Frank winced as he tried to turn round. "Folks don't leave bits o' wood lyin' around for long these days. Anyhow, why you askin'?"

c) From chapter 1 of *Falling Suns* by Julie-Ann Corrigan, in which Rachel and Liam's young son is still missing. The writing here is refreshingly clear.

I'd felt sorry for my old boss during last night's visit. It couldn't be easy for him to be heading up this particular investigation. He was like Joe's godfather. He'd wanted to say something positive, as he would have done easily with any other victim's mother; but with me my ex-boss became tragically inarticulate.

'Are you staying home today?' Liam's voice was tight and weary.

I hadn't heard him come through the patio door. His honey coloured hair was uncharacteristically unkempt; tufts jutted out from the top his head. His deep blue eyes seemed shrunken, and high, triangular cheekbones pressed outwards from the side of his face.

'I guess so,' I said, noticing the stubble that was growing into a beard. How could that happen in six days? And the absence of the scarf, which he'd remembered to leave in his den. 'Still reporters camped out at the bottom of the street. Gillespie managed to move them from the front of the house.'

'I know. That's good,' Liam said.

'I wish they'd piss off.'

He stood behind me and rubbed the tangled metal wires in my shoulder muscles, 'They're just doing a job.'

I turned my head, looking up at him. I smoothed his hand that still lay on the top of my shoulder. 'How's the new painting going?'

'It's not.'

'You shouldn't be working.'

'I know.' His hand stopped rubbing my muscles. 'We have to talk, Rachel.'

Now was the time. Liam was offering me my chance to assuage at least some guilt.

Chapter 35

The Climax

Time for the defibrillator or go for a snooze?

I recently read a thriller (the first in a planned series) by a new author where 30+ pages at this crucial stage were devoted to a detailed explanatory backstory. This negated all the previous tension and momentum, so in the end, I lost the will to live.

I do occasionally wonder if some editors are literally out to lunch, and the rise in self-published, often poorly edited work, seems to be adding to these disappointments. The fastidious editor of the old school is I fear, a dying species. I was lucky.

The chiller thriller's climax should be a dramatic, unforgettable point in the story where, between here and the ending, could come a surprise or two or a major twist. Where the reader will realise all has not been as it seemed. Perhaps someone involved in an ongoing sub-plot, emerges with a shocking truth. Perhaps, the enemy is cornered in an exceptionally dangerous place. Perhaps, especially if your book is a standalone, your main character has been the real enemy who's been leading *even you* up the garden path. That's when writing so-called 'fiction' gets scary.

The climax to the terrifying *House of Leaves*, is set in its 'Black Room' that mysteriously appears, but I won't spoil your pleasure by revealing more!

Exercise

Can you recall at least one exciting chiller thriller climax? If yes, why has it stayed in your mind? Had the tension built up to boiling point? Had the life of the main protagonist hung in the balance? Identifying why the climax was memorable, will help your own writing.

Example

a) From the climax of my Gothic chiller, *The Yellowhammer's Cradle*, when Janet Lennox another servant girl at Ardnasaig House, is betrayed not only by her friend Linnet Garvie, but even her own brother.

"Where's Miss Garvie?" asked the constable whose normally stiff moustache drooped either side of his mouth. "We sent her up to get a confession from you."

Janet could hardly speak, and when she did, the words felt like lumps of old bannock in her mouth. "I never saw her. I've nothing to confess. And *she's* the witch. Not me." She turned to see Falcon Steer's melting brown eyes hard as glass. She registered a swift movement alongside. The blur of the rifle butt lifted upwards.

Crack.

Her skull.

Crack.

Her ribs.

Voices, images fading as she fell.

"Ye wean's wee vertebra," called out Coyle triumphantly. "And your tale of Duns just another wicked lie…"

Plop.

"The gutting knife ye used for all your crimes."

Plop.

"Yer mother's eyes."

Plop.

"Your diary. Your brother's letter." Said the minister.

Plop.

They tore the boots from her feet, the clothes from her limbs and the chilly morning air stung her bare, goose-pimpled body.

"Pickings here," someone said. "Thirty pounds…"

"I'll ha' that. I'm next of kin."

Calum? No…

The rope ripped into her neck.

"Tighter...tighter..."

Blackness, whiteness. Calum's voice again. Tall as a tree, he looked down at her.

"She's heavy," he smiled. "I should ken."

Plead your belly...

"And we ken why."

Up, up, the sharp rub of stones on her skin, then the suck of iced water in her closing throat. That dead March midnight all over again...

"Go lie wi'me bairn and whatever else is feeding in yer belly," Calum again. The one who'd loved her too much.

"Up she comes. Hold it..."

"Right. Down she goes. Getting the hang o' this now. 'Tis time that blue vein in her forehead was of use to us."

"Up!" A crown of bones in her hair. The one from her corset, sticking up like a mast.

"Down!" Till her numb toes touched silt, then the top of her mother's bible and what remained of that other soul, gone before, gurning his own wee welcome.

Chapter 36

Ending It All

Remember your reader will be turning over 250+ pages of your chiller thriller, so it's only fair to reward them with an ending that's both realistic and satisfying. A common cop-out is the *Deus ex Machina* device of bringing in an unlikely and artificial element to the proceedings. This fools no one. Endings should neither drag on after the climax, nor be stuffed with expository afterthoughts and rationales. This can be another kiss of death.

IT WAS ALL A DREAM?... If so, I'm sorry, but put your manuscript in the re-cycling bin immediately!

HAPPY OR SAD ENDINGS?

Americanreaders, I was told by my agent, enjoy 'happy endings.' Yet for all of us, unless you believe in the Resurrection, the transmigration of souls or whatever else, everything on this mortal coil, ends with death. And life itself a series of adjustments to deaths along the way. However, in crafting fictional endings for our loyal readers, we can still employ justice, redemption, emotional closure and sew up those remaining threads which, if left dangling, risk these readers feeling short-changed. But happy? Is this *your* book or not? How much (especially if a first novel) do you want to be published? It's a hard call.

My first two published chillers were subject to considerable editorial input from both agent and editor, which, with other subsequent editors, diminished during the past decade. It was a steep, but valuable learning process. To the novice, I'd say, trust them, go with the flow and avoid being labelled as a 'tricky' author. The time will come when you will have more autonomy.

GLAD TO BE RID, OR FEELING BEREAVED?

Ending a book can trigger emotional extremes in the writer. It's been a gut-wrenching marathon. A journey of a lifetime. I was kept in hospital for nine days after our first daughter was born, but no such pampering for you! Already you may have a sequel mapped out with chilling plans for perhaps a character who still has unfinished business. And of course, there's the editing…

Exercises

i)   Study specifically the endings of at least 3 published chiller thrillers. Do they work for you? If so, why?

ii) If not, why?

iii) Explore at least 4 possible endings for your own book, given what has transpired in the climax. There is still room for a twist, but it should stem from what's already in place.

Examples

a) From my recently finished thriller, *Carcass*, second in the trilogy featuring ex DI John Lyon who's just back from the Poitou region. He's investigated the abduction of a young boy and a racehorse from west Wales, and still holds a flame for DC Alison McConnell, his former colleague in Nottingham CID who'd used some of her leave to help him. But it's not only summer that's coming to an end…

We sat together at a pub bench-style table and benches outside *Burnside's* warm, south-facing front wall. With the sun still climbing, the dark copse beyond their largest field being grazed by another farmer's sheep, resembled the one beyond the carp lake at *Les Tourels*. Ominous and brooding.

The older collie dog had settled himself between our feet. The end of his fine tail occasionally flicking as if in some dream. As for Alison, she looked wonderful. Her auburn hair tied up in the same clasp she'd worn during our fateful trip to west Wales that seemed so long ago. Her cheeks tanned, and those close-fitting jeans leaving just enough to the imagination. And yet there was still that same adversarial tone as she'd used during the Enquête in Poitiers. The sense I'd let her down. Let Laure down...

"Who'll be looking after Mathieu?" she asked, pouring out black coffee from the full cafetière. "You said yourself he's been unhappy in that foster home since he heard about his real Dad being dead."

"Nothing's been finalized, but there's still a chance he could go back to *Ty Capel*."

"What?" Her eyes widened in horror. "Surely not?"

"Alain Deschamps *is* part of his family."

"Only through marriage." She leaned forwards, letting the sunlight deepen her cleavage between her shirt lapels. "Besides, he's blind. So... so... why not us?"

Jesus...

I could imagine Mathieu's weird teenage sister Laure in the psychiatric hospital convincing everyone she was a model inmate and being released early. Mistakes did happen. A lot. I'd seen the consequences.

I shivered, while overhead, clouds that had suddenly appeared as if from nowhere, began separating then joining, blocking out the sun and dulling the colors of the land. I shivered again, watching a buzzard appear and hover over that same busy field, searching for prey.

"Is that what you and Ben would have done?" I tested her. "Gone for an instant family?"

I made her look at me, and not until that buzzard had swooped to snatch up something small that wriggled and screamed in its grasp, did I realize how deep the wound of her affair still was. For both of us.

"He's dead. Don't be so bloody cruel."

"I'm sorry." But I wasn't.

"And if you'd showed some empathy with Laure, she might have been more forthcoming earlier on. Look how she was. A coiled, angry spring. My God, if someone had made *me* have a child I didn't want, or wouldn't have had a hope in Hell of looking after..."

Her voice trickled away on the breeze as I left the table and made my way down to my car. The buzzard gone to find another meal. As for me, I'd go and phone my sister. She'd said she could do with some company down in Collioure. Still missing her late husband.

And when I reached the road, I glanced back to see that Alison and the dog had gone, and in their place hovered a rain cloud's slowly-shifting shadow.

Note; There is, as Americans would say, some 'closure' here to shocking events, but I wanted to show the reader that John Lyon isn't a man to be easily brought down. Not even by the woman he'd loved, who'd also risked her life with him in France. That he'll live to see another day.

b) The ending to *The Yellowhammer's Cradle* - awaiting submission - where the ambitious, ruthless, but ultimately cowardly Catriona McPhee who framed Janet Lennox, has been finally cornered.

Only the sounds of the blackthorn spitting and cracking in the grate, broke the quietude after she'd finished. Whether or not the two constables believed her compulsion to rid the dead house-keeper of Isobel Baird's eyes, was hard to tell, as neither had spoken. Not even those two liars, Iain McPhee and Fergus Bogle.

"May I change out of these wet clothes?" she'd asked at last.

"Two minutes," said the officer called Watson and, while her father sat slumped in a chair, head in hands before their joint trip to Inverary Gaol, Catriona left the room. But the air, instead of getting warmer towards the next landing seemed even colder, bearing a strange, rotting smell which intensified as she kept on climbing.

Past her dead step-brother's locked sanctuary and the architect's quarters with its useless double bed. Into his wife's room to snatch the portrait and carry it up to what had once been her attic room. She felt a stranger there all over again, her sodden stockinged feet still leaving their damp imprint on the wooden floor behind her. Her pulse oddly steady

That stink from the laundry room was stronger now, but she had other things on her mind. Having laid the portrait of Isobel Baird glass side up, she stamped on it once, twice, until the glass split and splintered, tearing through her stockings and into her own skin, bringing vivid red sprays of blood that obliterated that vengeful woman's face.

She was thirteen all over again, back in Footer's Cottage, trapped by more than bad weather as that poor crow's body had hit the window. The thud. The way it had fallen...

At least it was free. Unlike her.

"Did ye know that last September, me son had been left everything? All written down in black and white?"

Nothing was worth turning round for. Not even her father. He'd followed her up here to torment her again.

"So how does that make ye feel, having driven him to freeze himself in the loch?"

"Go away."

"I will. And when Falcon Steer's payment arrives for ye, I'll take it to build my ane son the best braw grave in Argyll. Ye see daughter, to my mind, ye've had too much already."

With her feet sticking to the floor, she heaved up the small sash window letting the snow hit her face, her neck, her arms as she squeezed her upper body and the rest of her through beyond the eaves.

Fly...

As she flew, trailing her own blood behind her, she glimpsed again those mossy hollows inlaid with blue, blue eyes, watching her from amidst the lime trees' branches. Isobel Baird's white jaw bone of perfect teeth opened in a smile, while below, a pony and trap rattled up the carriageway, bearing two men - a stranger and the husband whose pale, uncomprehending face was, for a fleeting moment, lost in darkness.

Note; This young woman who'd happily connived in the death of a fellow servant girl who'd stood in the way of her dream of becoming wife to the Laird of Ardnasaig House, is a product of her time and class, where jobs were scarce and the only chance of betterment was to move away. However, her father, hardly whiter than white, having had a lengthy affair with Isobel Baird, has betrayed her. One could ask, which is the worst crime?

Chapter 37

How Have Your Main Characters Changed By The End?

It's important that they do.

Exercise

In a detached way, take each of your main characters in turn, and analyse how events and personalities have altered their views and behaviour. E.g., a mother may now hate her own son. A former criminal may be helping disadvantaged kids... If you realise that no-one has changed, or if that change is barely noticeable, then take another look.

Examples

a) In *A Night With No Stars*, Lucy, who against all the odds, wanted to stay on at her new house near Rhayader, has decided to leave.

b) From *Overspill* where Rita Martin, mother of the murdered Jez, learns from DI Tim Fraser that Frank, her unreliable, easily manipulated husband, is lost at sea. Although she's recently grown closer to Sgt. Tim Fraser, her feelings for Frank still remain. His problem - he was all too human.

"Whatever," said Fraser. "This guy Donnelly's one seriously nasty piece of work. Did Frank ever mention him to you?"

"No, but might have done tonight. You see, he was supposed to be coming over to talk to me about things. Said he'd made a Will and got something for the kids. You and him were also going to meet and to be honest, I was dreading it."

"When did he tell you that?" Fraser looked across at her. The woman he loved was less than a metre away and now he should get up and take her in his arms. But his body was too rooted in the day's grim memories and they weren't over yet.

"This morning. He rang up."

"How could he think of getting back? He was on the bloody ferry..."

"Ferry?" Rita interrupted, trying to make sense of it all.

"Yes. The *St. Christopher*. It was stuck near France till half twelve today because of a customs strike."

"Maybe he thought he could still get here," said Rita. "Anyhow, he left me a message later. He couldn't make it after all."

"My God.'

"What d'you mean, my God?"

Silence, before Fraser cleared his throat.

"Look, I did my best, Rita. You've got to believe that. I tried to reach him, I really did." He glanced at the biscuit packet again. This was unbearable.

"Reach him? What's going on? Is he alright?" She had no mental picture of events down south and nothing was making sense. If Fraser was trying to spare her feelings he was having the opposite effect.

"Jarvis and I caught him fighting with this Donnelly bloke. Frank tried to get away and climbed on to the top deck rail..."

"So where's he now? Can I see him?"

Another silence and a moment's panic passed like electricity between them.

"You can't."

"Why?"

Fraser sucked in his breath as if he needed every last drop of it for what was coming next. "I couldn't find him after..."

"After what?"

"He fell into the water. Rita, I'm so bloody sorry."

She felt sick and faint, the kitchen around her beginning to move as Frank loomed up larger than life in her mind. His crinkly hair, his outdoor skin. The way he'd let himself go before all this business...

"D'you mean you went in after him?" she asked finally.

"It was no big deal. I had to, while there was still a chance of rescuing him."

A numb silence followed, hard to break, but in which Rita now realised the courage of the man slumped opposite her.

"Thank you doesn't sound much of a word, does it?"

"I don't want thanks, Rita. He was part of you, part of the kids..." Fraser felt tears begin to prick his own eyes. He tried pulling himself together, just then needing more than ever to feel her close, but still unable to move.

"Did anyone else help look for him?" she asked, for the idea of no body was unbearable. It was impossible.

"Been at it all day. Choppers the lot."

A brief pause followed suddenly broken by Freddie calling out again in his sleep. Fraser instinctively turned towards the passageway.

"Frank never learnt to swim, you know," Rita began. "Even when Jez started at the baths. It was like pulling teeth trying to even get him near the place..." Her voice tailed away into a void of bleakness and sorrow. Referring to Frank now was almost too painful and she squeezed her eyes shut with no real urge to reopen them.

Note; No-one's character is black and white. Certainly not those of these two characters who realise the rest of their lives will be quite different from what's been before. Meanwhile, a psychopathic young serial killer is still at large, and Rita still wants justice for her son's needless death.

Chapter 38

To Epilogue Or Not?

If you have already included a Prologue in your chiller thriller, an Epilogue or Afterword or similar, can complement this, by rounding off the novel in a rather more elegiac way, which can contrast with the necessary pace of the ending. It can also spring one last surprise.

Exercises

i) Read how other writers have written their Epilogues. What's your verdict? Tacked on, or meaningful?

ii) Try writing half a page of your own possible Epilogue. If you then feel it doesn't add anything, then fine. But you might find it creates another layer to your narrative by giving more 'closure.'

Examples

a) The Epilogue's first section from *The Nighthawk.* in which Ex-DI John Lyon is still living a nightmare.

EPILOGUE

September 12th 1987 12.30 pm.

Most nights, here at The Grange, I lie awake still haunted by the events of last spring. I'm either by the Bayrou again, in that oppressive stillness broken by rustling bamboos, bursts of rifle fire and the sudden shriek of some startled bird. Or else plunging from that roaring chopper into deep snow to save the one woman I loved.

As every bloody sleeping remedy under the sun has proved useless, I'm now on happy pills. Four a day. Better that than joining Ben Rogers, I tell the nurse who dishes them out.

Meanwhile, since my first visit to the patients' library here, I've started enjoying poetry again since my schooldays. It's T.S. Eliot's 'Burial Ground' that speaks to me the most. The first three lines...'April is the cruelest month,' especially.

And so it proved.

Sometimes I ask my shrink when it will be that I can go back to my flat, drive my car and be normal again, but her reply is always "when we feel you're ready."

That's the trouble in a place like this. No-one listens. No-one really understands. But worse is, despite the comfortable accommodation, my pulse habitually quickens in fear.

Two lads are larking around on the cricket pitch just beyond the hospital grounds. I could open my window just the few inches I'm allowed, and shout out to them to fuck off, but not now. Oh no. Definitely not now. Getting involved is for other fools.

I'm just wondering where would be a better place to display my two railway remnants from Dansac, when a shrill ringing fills the room.

"A man called Brishen Petsha, from Toulouse," says our new receptionist coming through on the Cellnet phone that Carol and George have so generously just sent me. "Wherever that is. I can hardly make out what he wants," she complains. "Would you like me to transfer the call to your new toy?"

"Yes. Of course," I say.

Suddenly, it's as if a towering black wave is looming close by, but when he begins by apologizing for troubling me, and hoping my health is improving, I press my ear to the unfamiliar receiver in the hope of hearing some small trace of Mireille in his voice. Her innocence and eagerness, but there's only age and grief, in a dialect I'm struggling to grasp.

b) In *Office For the Dead*, DI Martin Webb returns from his investigations in the south of France to make a final, shocking discovery. His boss...

EPILOGUE

Happisburgh. Norfolk. Sunday 31st October.

Sunday bells and a calm lulling tide on the wane. Martin's dry-cleaned jacket still smells of damp and blood as he sits on the caravan steps with his third Marlboro Light of the day and letters from Gabriel Victoire and Gaia Balesta in his pocket. At least Gabriel is on the mend and Jean-Marie has come home. But it's different here. There's been another fight. Dora's begged him not to return to France for Guy Legrange's trial. She argues there's too much unrest between the Far Right there and the cities' ghettoes. Especially in Toulouse and Marseille.

He's used words like duty and obligation, yet fears the worst as he watches the sea and sky almost merge until a breeze picks up, almost imperceptibly, bringing froth to the little waves, and the sense that a storm might be brewing.

It's time to act.

His boots sink into the deep dry sand near the shallow cliffs, through the detritus left by the current until they reach water. Having dug into his jeans pocket and found the Beretta he's kept for too long, a long throw followed by the sound of closure as it vanishes and then, as if war is declared overhead, a roar moves in from the east. The sea rises up as his ears choke with din. He runs back the way he came, up the coastline's ravaged defenses and along the grass to the white hive where she sleeps curled up on her side until the dust devil strikes the shore, lifting swathes of sand high into the sky like so many veils, toppling those lighter, unoccupied caravans to the ground.

In the aftermath, they venture outside in the silence and, together with other hardy souls on a pre-winter break, check the cracked, empty shells of Downlea, Seaspray and the like before turning to the beach where a crater lies beneath the cliffs. Where incongruous things trapped inside it, catch his eye. He insists she stay safe with their unborn child, while he slides down the displaced sand to the beach and advances towards what the tornado has exposed. No rocks or boulders, these. No child's toys abandoned from the summer, but a dark green Black & Decker power saw, fleshy limbs, hair, and blood the color of old liver. A man's head, face down. Neatly severed above the atlas bone. Someone he recognizes, with a small yellow shell wedged protectively in his left ear, as if to spare him any more grief.

Chapter 39

Your Title

Make it unforgettable!

It's a good idea to have a working title in mind before you've written the last line of your book. It would have arisen from the material you were dealing with, and may well be the one that stays. However, it pays to keep an open mind, because the wrong title can kill a book dead. The right one affects it positively in every way by heightening and distilling the content at the same time. It can become an indelible stamp to the agent or editor who sees it, and later, if published, the reading public's mind. If original enough, it's less likely to spawn lookalikes. However, before making a final decision check yours isn't identical or too similar to those of other publications. Google the word/s and check on Amazon Books etc.

Having decided on *Come and Be Killed*, with my publishers also liking it for its nursery rhyme origins, I discovered that the very same had been used on a crime novel just ten years previously. I'm now much more wary, and check out the internet first.

Single word titles are currently popular, and perhaps easier to continue with for a series than those beginning with Dead or Angels etc. which present a daunting task to their author. *Sabbathman* is spot-on for Graham Hurley's gripping political thriller set in London and Northern Ireland, where the assassinations take place on Sundays.

Jo Nesbo's *Nemesis*, *Headhunters* and *Phantom* create powerful associations, while Suzanne Ruthven's chiller, *Whittlewood* suggests perfectly what's in the tin. The title of my latest thriller, *Malediction*, means 'a curse,' which I hope gives a clue as to its controversial content. *Dominion* by C.J. Sansom, whose historical thrillers address the abuse of power, is a good fit for his recent

WWII political thriller, while Adrian Magson's forthcoming taut spy thriller featuring ex-MI5 Harry Tate is aptly entitled *Execution*.

I hope you found this short list helpful, showing that it pays the author to look a little further than the obvious. When I'd finished writing what would become my first published chiller, I'd called it *Snare,* and was happy with that. Why? Because everywhere I'd looked on that doleful part of the Fens where the river Nene divides Lincolnshire from Norfolk, there was killing a-plenty. Seals being shot out at sea, herrings trapped in vast nets, beakless broilers incarcerated in huge, galvanised iron sheds, etc. etc.

However, I began reading Hilaire Belloc's *Hills and The Sea* collection of travel essays and found one relating to that very region, where he'd waited half a day with his bicycle on Sutton Bridge (which spans the river Nene) for the man laboriously cleaning it with a rag to finish, until...

"... We all stepped over into the Wringland. "

That last word sent a shiver down my spine, and I began to research it. Lo and behold, I discovered 'Wringland came from the old English 'Wringen,' related to old High German 'Ringan' and the Gothic 'Wrungo' meaning Snare.'

Coincidence or what?

No-one I spoke to in those flatlands had heard of this name, but it didn't matter. I knew I'd found my title, and fortunately, my agent and editor liked it too.

Two word titles can also be ideal. Caroline Carver's great eco-thriller *Black Tide* took place off the coast of Australia. John Grisham's *The Bretheren* has the right air of menace. *The Testimony* by James Smythe, in which the voice of God should not be ignored.

Three word titles give even more scope, but again should reflect the pace, mood and the chiller thriller's main thrust. Mary Higgins Clark's titles usually do the business too. A masterful plotter with a huge following. *The Lost Years; I'll Walk Alone* certainly holds an air of mystery.

The four word title, *Close To The Bone* by Stuart McBride, is chillingly perfect. As for me, I chose *Behold A Pale Horse* with its strong Templar and WWII strands, because Death 'rode upon him.' In fact, Death is everywhere.

Longer titles seem popular in literary fiction and even 'cosy' crime, but don't sit quite so easily in the thriller genre where pace and a build-up of suspense are key. If you are self-publishing, take the advice of people you trust. Brainstorm and bounce ideas off your more reliable contacts. Whoever is printing your book for you, may also be helpful. But whatever your situation, 'is my title the best it can be?' should be your nagging question.

Exercises

i)   What's the prevailing mood of your chiller thriller?

ii) What's the most frightening event that happens in it?

iii) Choose 6 nouns which sum up this event. E.g., if there's a crucifixion, (as in *Cold Remains*) even an upside-down one, could Cross play a part? If cannibalism, then perhaps flesh, meat, bone or some other bodily component could play a part?

iv) Choose the best.

v)   Using search engines and a Thesaurus to find another 6 possible alternatives to this particular word.

vi) Try the Oxford Dictionary of quotations as well. Shakespeare is a bottomless pit of inspiration!

Chapter 40

Your Name

You've named your characters with care, but what about you? An author name is an important part of the 'package.' Several well-published thriller authors prefer initials + a surname. M.R. Hall, C.J. Sansom, R.N. Morris, etc. This neutralises gender and sounds businesslike. For dark and taut content, the names Harlan Coban and Jo Nesbo are tailor-made, unlike Priscilla Fotheringay-Shawcross.

Lee Child, with his one syllable per name suggests economy and pace. And as for Karen Slaughter? Well, you couldn't make that up.

My maiden name is Wolff, but my first editor preferred the alliteration of both the 'S' of my first name and married name. However, my current editor at Sparkling Books did consider at one point that I choose another for *Malediction* because of its controversial theme. Common practice too, when an author changes genre or they (or on their publisher's advice) want to re-invent themselves. When Michael Ridpath finished writing his financial thrillers, he chose a pseudonym to attract a new publisher for his brilliant Icelandic series.

Ruth Rendell, crime writer becomes Barbara Vine for her psychological thrillers. Saga-writer, Catrin Collier, is Katherine John for her crime novels. There are many other examples. So, it may pay you to check out several author names and consider if a *nom de plume* might be more effective for you too.

Exercises

i) Check out thriller writers' names, including those using alliteration, initials; the letters 'o' and 'u' in particular; also single syllable names.

ii) Make up at least 4 possible pseudonyms for yourself.

iii) Check on Amazon etc. that they've not already been taken.

Chapter 41

The Synopsis

Aka The Writers' Curse!

But it needn't be. However, its function is to help 'sell' your book and inform a potential agent or editor what it's about, so the most important information should come first. E.g., Genre/Where and when set/Timespan/Word count. This last item is vital as some publishers won't even look at anything longer than 100,000. Some 80,000. Even 60,000.

A quotation or 'shout line' repeated from the manuscript and placed under the heading, can also add atmosphere.

Your synopsis should show characters' full names in capital letters, and give their ages. It should echo the mood and tone of your novel and ideally include some pivotal dialogue too, although I've always found this tricky. Generally, a synopsis can be either one or three pages long and always reveal the ending. (Check agents'/publishers' requirements first before submitting) Also state if you are considering creating a future series or a trilogy as in Steig Larssen's political thrillers and Lee Child's ongoing Jack Reacher books, this can be a tempting proposition.

Exercises

i) Good guides on writing synopses can often be found in various writing magazines. Nicola Morgan has written an excellent one, *How To Write a Great Synopsis*. Also, check out the *Writers' &Artists' Yearbook*.

ii) Try writing a synopsis for your chiller thriller. Read it aloud, and persevere with editing until it covers the plot and shows how, by the end, your main characters have changed.

Example

a) My synopsis for *The Yellowhammer's Cradle*.

Synopsis of THE YELLOWHAMMER'S CRADLE 96,000 words

An historical Gothic thriller set mainly during the winter of 1851 in rural Argyll, where superstition and fear of witchcraft still lurk amongst the moss and the heather; where even the sweetest of faces conceals an evil heart.

13-year old CATRIONA McPHEE dreams of working of at Ardnasaig House on the shores of Loch Nonach, and to one day replace the still-missing ISOBEL BAIRD. But her father IAIN forbids it because he guards a terrible secret which could cost both their lives. He witnessed her strangle his lover, angered by his trysts with her while her mother MARI still clung to life. Little did CATRIONA know this woman was ISOBEL BAIRD.

Defying him, she's eventually hired by ISOBEL'S only son JAMES (18 yrs) His architect father DONALD is due to return from the Crimea for Christmas. However, JANET LENNOX (also 18 yrs) and MARGARET, her housekeeper mother view this beguiling newcomer with suspicion. Rivalry soon builds between the two girls who vie for the feckless JAMES'S favours.

Two years before, in Greenock, JANET, pregnant by her soldier brother CALUM was urged by 'wise woman' LINNET GARVIE, to drown the newborn. JANET used the well at Ardnasaig House, but remains guilt-ridden. As days pass, handyman FERGUS BOGLE, who witnessed this, seems to forge a bond with CATRIONA before he vanishes.

He loved the architect's wife, who never returned from her loch side walk with her two dogs, and when CATRIONA steals her ivory comb he's kept as a souvenir, he resolves to trap her - 'the Yellowhammer' - and her colluding father. He also sees her stab a Clearances victim in the forestry, and attack the man's dog which once belonged to ISOBEL.

Coquettish CATRIONA will stop at nothing to oust plain JANET from her post, but is shocked to recognise ISOBEL from a new portrait brought to the house; as the very woman she'd strangled when she was just twelve. CATRIONA assumes her father will protect her forever.

Wrong.

Suspecting that JANET might be pregnant by JAMES, she spreads rumours about her and butchers the already dead MARGARET. DONALD returns home for Christmas and falls for her while JANET is taken for questioning.

A mysterious stranger, FALCON STEER is LINNET'S brother, to whom JANET has confided her guilty secret about drowning her baby. Both are on a witch hunt after his small daughter died having met JANET who escapes custody to find JAMES. She finds him dead on a nearby crannog, having killed himself in remorse over his spinelessness during her unjust treatment.

Knowing of CATRIONA'S crimes from FERGUS, she returns to a seemingly deserted Ardnasaig House for her hidden wages before leaving for good. However, her enemies lie in wait. Even CALUM won't save his own sister from a slow drowning in the well, where she's reunited with their drowned baby's bones.

CATRIONA, who realises DONALD BAIRD is infertile and now of no use, is captured by FERGUS and her father. He betrays her to save his own skin. Both are forced to dig up ISOBEL'S skeleton from inside a mud-filled rowing boat. But before they are gaoled, CATRIONA, upon learning that JAMES was in fact, her father's love-child with ISOBEL, throws herself from her attic window and dies.

Chapter 42

What Visuals Can Enhance My Chiller Thriller?

Anything visual that enlivens your pages will always add to the cost of publishing.

That said, I personally like to see imagery and text in any book I read.

In his superb political thriller, *Sabbathman*, Graham Hurley uses Downing Street's Security Office emblem several times at the start of certain chapters. They make a powerful starting point. Minette Walters used many examples of record books, notices and reports, all to add variety to the text. Other thriller authors such as Suzanne Ruthven, use interesting and relevant symbols to embellish their chapter numbers or first letter. Johan Theorin adds photographs, while Mark Z. Danielewski's disturbing imagery makes his *House of Leaves* even more frightening.

Diary excerpts, other cryptic fragments can add yet more interest. Sarah Rayne's *Spider Light* has the most creepy, claustrophobic, hand-drawn map at its start, which sets the tone perfectly. *Cloven* too, begins with 1830 maps of Nether Wapford village in south Northamptonshire, and Lampeter in Cardiganshire. I drew them myself and am still grateful to Pan Macmillan for agreeing to their inclusion, also for allowing Lilith Leakes' strange, 22 page 'Diary' to be added to *Wringland*.

If you're planning to use visuals in a self-published e-edition of your book, it's best to seek professional advice beforehand.

Exercises

i) Explore what other thriller writers have done to visually enhance the reader experience.

ii) Write down what kinds of imagery might possibly benefit

your material.

iii) Can *your* chapter headings contain an interesting symbol of some kind?

iv) A visit to the graphic design department in any nearby Higher Education establishment could well be useful. A student may, as part of their portfolio, and for a modest fee, help with ideas suitable for reproduction. Worth an ask!

Chapter 43

Editing

The really creative part of it all.

Exercises

i) Print out a hard copy of your already partially checked manuscript (see Section 33.) and read through, still keeping in mind the Twelve Commandments listed at the start of this book. They are the result of all the sound input and advice I've received over the past decade, and from my own steep learning curve.

ii) Next, work through this first draft text, line by line, excising out all 'padding' words, sloppy clichés (unless deliberate,) unwanted repetitions, redundant adverbs, adjectives and the like. Punctuation glitches too, which seem to always slip under the radar. You may have to re-organise your material by cutting here and there. Perhaps by re-arranging chapters to get the sequencing right and the pace kept up. All in a good cause!

iii) Go back to your pc. with notes you've made, and systematically work through them all to create your second draft. This should give you a lift. Your book is taking shape.

iv) Print this copy out. Yes, I know printing ink costs, but the screen can seduce the eye.

v) Keep pecking away until your final draft - which may even be number 6 or more - is the best it can be.

vi) Check other published books to see where new chapters begin, and why. Even if at first, they seem unconnected with those immediately around them, the bigger picture will soon emerge.

Example

a) How would you edit this short passage?

Rio de Janeiro had until recently been just a name in her school geography books but not any more for here under her hot sticky feet even the short dusty walk towards the airport terminal threatened to melt her skin and blind her eyes with salty perspiration.

She quickly checked her sleek Gucci watch and for a moment its tiny silvery numbers seemed to vanish under the sun's midday glare.

b) Now can you see the difference?

Remember to frequently save your work on memory sticks and other foolproof devices while you're writing on your pc. Many's the time that portions of my work have vanished during a sudden power cut. Never be too carried away to press Save, then Save As...

Warning! A well-published crime writer had his house burgled, and his pc and all back-up material was stolen. The novel he'd almost finished for his contract had gone for good. A nightmare scenario, so do take these memory sticks etc. with you whenever you go out.

Chapter 44

Editorial S.O.S! Where To Go For More Help?

Certainly not your best friend or your uncle who's always wanted to write.

It's tempting to get in touch with a published writer who you've perhaps met at some literary event or other, and ask if they'd take a look at your finished book. This isn't always advisable, as they may be busy working to a deadline and also have other pressures. Besides, no request should come without the offer of a reasonable fee. No-one, least of all most writers, can afford to give their time and expertise for nothing. You will either be ignored, or suffer a sharp rebuke. However, some writers may be generous and genuinely want to see you succeed, so, with a fee established, start by sending the first 3 chapters and a synopsis. If posting, always include a correctly stamped, self-addressed envelope. If emailing, make sure you're not passing on a virus.

Manuscript Appraisers

The CWA's Crime Readers' Association, now offers a two-tier Manuscript appraisal service at reasonable rates for writers worldwide. This is proving highly successful and valuable, particularly as their prestigious Debut Dagger Award is for an author's first and unpublished crime/thriller. Entries come from all over the world.

One or two major publishers and bigger literary agencies are offering aspiring writers the chance to join their mentoring programmes. I've heard these come at a price, but may be worth it, if at the end, you are given a contract.

Authonomy is a friendly and supportive online writing community supported by Harper Collins. The most rated books receive attention from its editors.

The website www.the nextbigauthor.com holds competitions where the prize is a professional critique.

There are also many Literary Consultancies to help with the editing and polishing of your new book. Of these, The Literary Consultancy is well known and successful. Others include organizations and individuals with experience of the publishing industry. These include the excellent Famelton Writing Services, Hilary Johnson, Cornerstones, Words Worth Reading, etc.

Compare costs. Some don't come cheap. Check out the appraiser too, but don't forget the benefits of a well-run writers' group where you can regularly read excerpts of your work to like-minded people. If joining an online community, take care with your copyright. Also, subscribe to a reliable writing magazine E.g., *The New Writer, Writing Magazine, Writers' Forum* or *Mslexia* (women writers only) that don't advertise vanity publishers, but do offer useful editorial guidelines, articles and notices. *TNW's* monthly e-newsletter is another mine of information and opportunities.

Finally, the *Writers' &Artists' Yearbook* or the *Writers' Handbook* should prove invaluable. You'll need an updated copy as agencies and publishers are in constant flux.

Exercises

i)   Use your internet search engines to find more mentoring and editorial services for fiction writers.

ii)   Select three; discover all about them and compare costs.

Chapter 45

Who'll Add A Few Kind Words?

Whether you're published by a mainstream or small, independent publisher or even self-published, anyone who can enhance your title, is always worth approaching.

Some six weeks before your chiller thriller is out there, your publisher's publicist will ask if any of your writerly contacts - preferably known and ideally, well-known, who write within or review the thriller chiller genre - could oblige with an eye-catching quote. Most well- published authors are willing to help the debut writer on their way by reading a proof copy, especially if their name and quote will appear on the final cover.

You and or your publicist must be shameless, but as I've advised earlier, nicely so. It also helps if you've attended relevant book launches, posted good reviews of your supporter's work online under your real name. Twittered and used your Face Book page to do the same, and if a reviewer has helped you out, praise their latest review.

Your publicist will cleverly sift the best parts of any mixed review to feature on your cover. Creative writing isn't just reserved for your own pages!

Net Galley (mentioned again in Section 53) is an online facility where a particular galley proof copy can, for six months, be downloaded free for reviewers. This is an extremely useful means for publishers to find keen reviewers. Ask your publicist. It's cheaper than sending out review copies. However, some reviewers still prefer to read a hard copy. If you are self-published, Twitter and Facebook are even more invaluable and not only for self-promotion. They'll also provide possibilities for reviews and quotes. More on these later. Meanwhile, etiquette is the name of the game.

Exercises

i)   Make a list of at least 4 possible contacts you already know who might review your book

ii)   Either email or send them a card. Phone calls or texts may not be considered good etiquette, unless you know the contacts very well. Twitter or Facebook requests can come after several lead-in 'conversations.'

Chapter 46

Cover Story

Your chiller thriller's cover and the information it shares with potential readers matter hugely. It must stand out from the myriad others on show, and ensnare the undecided reader. I've spent time in bookshops and libraries watching browsers checking books by well-known and unknown authors alike. First comes the front cover, its shout line and best quotes, then the back where more quotes and the blurb or pitch, can usually be found. (If a hardback this is generally inside the front cover.)

If the potential reader is hooked by the title, imagery and glowing quotes which promise a thrilling experience, they head for the till or the library counter. However, even readers faithful to a particular well-known author, can be turned off by an indifferent cover and title and the rest. They can also be turned off later by a cover that doesn't represent the story. So it's worth getting these elements right.

For those readers searching online, other factors come into play, notably reviews. Potential buyers do feel reassured by good ratings. We are all human.

If not self-publishing, your publisher may well suggest what cover design they feel is most appropriate and hopefully give you a choice in the matter. If not, you have to defer, and hope for the best. As I've mentioned earlier, don't be labelled a tricky author. The time will come when you'll have more say.

Exercises

If self-publishing, you can use your own photograph/artwork for a cover design or buy very reasonably from online photograph/graphics banks e.g., iStock. However, don't be tempted to use a photograph or image that may still be in copyright.

i) See what other self-published authors have done. Check the image source.

ii) For your cover design, sketch or find other sources for 6 possible images and typefaces.

iii) Graphic design students are always looking to beef up their portfolios, and for a modest fee, could help you come up trumps.

Examples

a) David Pinner's chiller, *Ritual* has a striking woodcut image of a threatening Pagan creature. The text is uneven, reflecting the madness between its covers.

b) Sarah Rayne's *Spider Light* shows a haunting strand of light glowing in the penumbra. Echoing exactly the mood of this psychological thriller

c) A famous thriller writer was told by his publisher that a helicopter would have to be added to the cover design of what was intrinsically a man-woman love story set during the Irish Troubles. This, they reasoned, would make the book more appealing to male readers. One can mock this, but creating the right perceptions is vital to a book's success.

d) *Malediction's* cover shows a stark red cross against a black background. However, for the American market, this cross is to be replaced by a less overtly religious image, and the Prologue, depicting a homosexual act between two priests, also has to be cut.

e) C.J. Sansom has given Michael Jeck's *King's Gold* a great quote on the top of its front cover. And rightly so. The title, in a mediaeval-type font stands out in gold bas-relief. Above this, the brooding face of a knight in armour stares out, and below shows part of a dusty, dramatic battle scene which continues round to the back cover. The whole image is suffused with a green-gold light. Brilliant.

f) *Cold Remains'* uncompromising cover in sepia tones, shows a large full-frontal skull and various bones, while the typography is in a cold blue. A suitably chilling combination.

Shout Line

Designed to cause a frisson of excitement and fear. Every word counts!

Exercises

i) Find several shout lines on thriller covers. Do they entice you to read the book?

ii) Compose 4 possible shout lines for your own chiller thriller.

Examples

a) 'A death trap is set to spring.' *Wringland.*

b) 'A scream for vengeance into the night.' *Cloven.*

c) 'Where no-one will hear you scream.' *A Night With No Stars.*

d) *'The Holy Blood and the Holy Grail meets Pride and Prejudice,'* Is typical of how publishers present the reader-to-be with already familiar titles. These ludicrous comparisons often bear little relation to what's in the tin.

Chapter 47

Blurbs

This short, carefully constructed summary should convey the mood and content of your book, and is an important selling tool. So spend time on it. They should arouse anticipation and curiosity, without giving too much of the plot away. Fifty words is the norm, but this can vary. Most publishers' editors will think up their own blurbs, but you could still present them with ideas. And you'll definitely need one if self-publishing and for Kindle, etc.

Exercises

i) Check out as many blurbs as you can which are on chiller thrillers similar to yours. Identify which ones work and which don't. Why?

ii) Compose at least three for your own book and try them out on any other writer friends.

Examples

a) Blurb for my *Cold Remains*.

When Jason Robbins arrives at the eerie Heron House in deepest Carmarthenshire for a writing course, he soon meets its two weird servants who seem to exercise a sinister power over their scheming employer, Monty Flynn. Another newcomer is Helen Jenkins, ex-art student and reluctant cook, to whom Jason is instantly attracted.

Together they discover what dangers really lurk behind those ivy-clad walls. How the terrible post-war past bleeds into the present when the tormented soul of the young woman haunting them will stop at nothing to have her story told.

But is her version of events to be trusted? And at what cost to

Jason and Helen when they attempt to find out the truth?

b) From *The Chase* by Lorna Fergusson.

Buried deep in the heart of the woods of the Dordogne, a region steeped in dark history, lies Le Sanglier, once the hunting lodge of a dissolute nobleman.

Englishman Gerald Feldwick, ignorant of events that have transpired there, buys the house as a bolthole. He tells his wife Netty that in France they can start afresh. They can escape the unbearable pain of an event which is fracturing their marriage. He tells her they can put the past behind them.

Netty is not so sure.

Netty is right.

The Chase: the past will hunt you down

c) From *Cloven.*

Little has changed in the picturesque village of Cold Firton, where evil has thrived unhindered for centuries.

In February 1830, surly Tomos Richards reluctantly takes his 14-year-old mute and crippled sister, along with his drove, from Cardiganshire towards London, hoping to find a cure for her injuries. Siân's journey is beset by danger and cruelty and, after much of the drove is lost in a bog, she takes her chance to run away. Alone, save for her pony and her loyal dog, and desperate to return to Wales, she mistakenly arrives at Tripp's Cottage in Nether Wapford, where cholera has just taken hold.

Shifting to the present day, Ivan Browning, a 32-year-old pottery teacher, has escaped London to live in the same Tripp's Cottage. There, he begins to experience ghostly pleas for help… while unwittingly becoming the target of two wealthy local criminal gangs. For it seems his investigations into the cottage's haunted history is about to uncover a gruesome mystery that others want to keep buried deep.

d) From my *A Night With No Stars.*

Little does Lucy Mitchell realize that swapping her stressful London job as an editor's assistant, for a life of rural peace, will lead her into the murderous world of Ravenstone Hall in picturesque Radnorshire. When she buys a small property on the estate belonging to an inebriate, widowed ex-cop and begins investigating who butchered his wife and mother of two now adult sons some fourteen years ago, her life too, is in the greatest peril.

Who is lying? Whose account can be trusted? Because in that twilight world, marked out not by days but nights, a reign of madness has begun.

Chapter 48

A Rock And Other Hard Places

Agent? Publisher? Or going it alone? What to do with your polished manuscript?

As a first-time writer, I'd urge you to try and find an agent to represent you. They give advice and help with contracts, rights, and not least their editorial expertise and contacts within the industry. Without mine, I doubt if the cross-genre chiller, *Wringland* would have found a home so quickly, but she knew which editor wanted such a dark, paranormal chiller. (That it was marketed as Sci-Fi didn't matter to me at the time, but it does illustrate the publisher's need to pigeon-hole.)

Further down the line, you may find you and your agent's paths diverge, but that's in the future.

Obviously, the larger the agency, with different agents for different genres and scripts etc, the longer their client lists. Curtis Brown, Sheil Land, David Higham, et al. Nevertheless, check them out. I was represented by a sole agency, and the prompt attention and focus was extremely helpful. Keep your ear to the ground for new agencies starting up and wanting to build their lists with fresh talent. Not all may yet be listed.

Chapter One Promotions (London-based) regularly provide opportunities for new writers to meet agents and editors, but the big question I'm often asked is, 'do I select one agent to submit to, or cast my bread upon the waters?'

Cynical I know, but having been on the publishing roller-coaster for just over a decade, I'm inclined to say, 'look after Number One.' Submit to whoever best represents your genre. However, avoid the turn-off, generic letter by making your approach more tailored to each individual agency. When an agent has 'bitten' with a definite offer of a contract, you can then politely withdraw your manuscripts from the others. Yes, always politely. I was told more than once, 'be nice to everyone on the way up because you'll need them on the way down.'

London agents and editors in particular, often meet up socially, and it's possible your name may crop up from more than one. One hears of bidding wars for a particular author. Nice work if you can get it! Other equally keen and conscientious agents may live elsewhere, but that's no reason to discount them.

A clued-up agent will know where to send your manuscript, and which editor is looking for what. They'll be on top of the ever-shifting game. What is encouraging is top agent John Jarrold's optimism. A Fantasy/Sci-Fi specialist, he has, since 2007 "done 20 three and four book deals for debut novelists, and in the majority of cases for authors with nothing else published previously... which proves the line authors use about publishers only wanting to take on 'known bestsellers' is simply untrue."

There are a number of exciting, independent publishers who seem more prepared to take risks with new authors, than the big, often conglomerate houses. These include; Sparkling Books; Myrmidon; Snow Books; Legend Press, (whose annual Luke Bitmead Writers' Bursary also carries a publishing contract.) Cinnamon Press; Salt Publishing etc. etc. Writers in Wales have a number of Welsh publishing houses with interesting lists. Gomer, Parthian Books, Seren and Honno - for women writers connected to Wales. They, like Cinnamon Press, regularly hold competitions and opportunities for inclusion in their excellent anthologies.

On the subject of how to how to hook and agent, look no further than Nicola Morgan's *Dear Agent – Write the Letter that Sells Your Book*. The excellent reviews of this e-book say it all.

Selling yourself is one of the hardest things to do, but sell yourself you must! Everything, from your writing on the envelope and positioning of the stamps to your closing sentence in your covering letter, counts.

You are unique, so let this shine through.

I've often found that writing a short biography first can lay a good foundation for your covering letter. It's less daunting to simply lay out the bones of your life to date. You can then cut the less interesting bits and embellish those that mark you out as a serious and ambitious writer. End your letter by assuring the agent that you enjoy working to deadlines and, because a two book deal (or more) could be in the offing, that you are currently working on either the sequel in a series or another standalone.

Example

a) What Trudy Drücker doesn't say in the following letter is that she can't have children, or that she has an eating disorder triggered by this fact. She's talking up the positives. Making herself sound like an attractive and marketable writer, for whom writing truly is her life.

Dear Dominic Meade,

I have recently completed a paranormal/historical thriller *Black Shroud* set in northern Italy – the first in a series featuring a young, single female doctor whose principles and dogged curiosity put her and her close-knit family's lives at risk from those with dangerous secrets to hide in the past and present

I'm now seeking an agent to represent my work, and because your agency's client list includes several successful authors writing in the historical thriller genre, you are my first port of call.

I was born in Aberdeen in 1976 to a Scottish mother and a Belgian father with German origins. This combination of two very different people and events surrounding my European family during the last war, have subconsciously formed the subsoil for my writing. My interest lies with betrayal, and those who, against all the odds, seek the truth.

I work part-time in pediatric medicine and am married to an architect. We re-located to Brussels from London three years ago and also keep a small village house in the Dolomites.

My short stories have been published in several international anthologies and last month in Ellery Queen Mystery Magazine. Patricia Highsmith and Andrea Camillari are my inspirations. I sing and play violin in a string quartet. But my biggest ambition is for my writing. I am disciplined, enjoy working to deadlines and am eager to raise my game to become a regular best-seller.

I hope that you find the enclosed synopsis and first three chapters of *Black Shroud* to be of interest.

I look forward very much to hearing from you,

Yours,

Trudy Drücker

Exercise

Ask yourself, would you as an agent/publisher in a crowded market place, take a punt on this author, given what you've read?

Whether submitting to an agent or editor online or by post, read the small print. Get names right. If posting, always add a stamped, self-addressed envelope with the correct postage or your submission could be binned. Unless requested, don't use Recorded Delivery as this can be a nuisance at the other end. Always keep a copy of the work submitted, just in case.

If going it alone, you have a range of options in self-publishing. It's a tough world and getting tougher for the author, which is why even a number of perfectly good mid-list writers struggling perhaps to find another agent and/or publisher, are using the many reputable and reasonably-priced self-publishing companies. Author House, for example, produces quality books and provides a helpful service. The internet and word of mouth should help you find the best one for you. It's not vanity publishing, and can sometimes lead to being picked up by a mainstream publisher.

However, the biggest and most exciting developments are with e-books. Kindle and the like are your platforms to the whole world, where royalties from sales are approximately 70% compared to 25% and less offered by the majority of conventional publishers. *Strangers Waiting*, my collection of short stories is now Kindle. I paid a friend to help me format the material correctly, then created Salem Publishing and also set up a PayPal account. So far, no problems, and with concerted marketing, you too could be successful. One caveat - giving away your e-book sends out completely the wrong message. I'd never do it.

Hot off the press comes news of interactive e-books where endings can be altered. Where readers can participate even more than they would in computer games. Faber and Harper Collins in the UK are encouraging contemporary writers to create the next generation of experimental novels. We're living in exciting times. So think what you could do with a keen and clever software developer!

Exercises

i) Check out thriller author dedications and acknowledge-ments to their agent/editor. Those mentioned may be interested in yours.

ii) Try writing your biography. Keep it to one page.

iii) Use it to inspire your covering letter/email to an agent. Again, keep to one page maximum. Don't send.

iv) Leave it for 2 days and take another look. Read it aloud, and check neurotically for spelling/grammatical errors before emailing or posting.

v) If self-publishing, find 4 companies and explore their products and costs.

vi) If publishing in e-format, check out Kindle, Smashwords,

Nook, etc. Always get advice on formatting and copyright issues, if unsure.

Chapter 49

Presentation Of Text And Formatting To Perfection

First impressions can make or break your submission.

A publisher will have their own house style, but it's best if you play safe with the font and layout of your manuscript. Courier is the choice of some agents and publishers, but I prefer Times New Roman. Yes, this does add more words per page, thus risking slowing the reader down, but I've had no complaints so far. *In a Night With No Stars*, I used several different fonts as chapter headings, and was fortunately able to keep them. They can add extra costs.

In his ground-breaking *House of Leaves*, Mark Z. Danielewski uses a number of different fonts, even presenting some pages upside down, so the reader is even more physically involved in reading them. Mysteriously, the word 'house' is always printed in blue.

Whichever font you choose, size 12 is the norm, as is double-spacing and non-left justifying your text. Indent new paragraphs rather than leave gaps between them. Where there is a natural break, I'd suggest a * * * symbol. Inner thoughts can be italicized to distinguish them from the rest of the text. Your mission is to keep the story flowing and to avoid breaking the reader's experience by too many ellipses, unnecessary hyphens and excla-mation marks, which can appear amateurish.

Faded ink is a killer. A pristine submission on good quality paper marks you out as a serious writer. Some authors add their name and contact details to their book's title on each page. Unless asked for this information, I'd keep your pages free of clutter. As a manuscript appraiser, I do find this information distracting, but realise it reduces the chance of the manuscript going astray.

If, as is becoming more common, the work is to be sent online, follow instructions carefully and re-format your text if necessary to what is required.

No writer should pay any agent or publisher to read any of their novels. Alarm bells should ring if they do! Vanity publishing sadly, still continues to operate under a variety of clever disguises.

Again, there are a number of reference books to help you. Please see the list at the end.

Exercises

i) Try both Courier and Times New Roman 12 on the same piece of writing. Choose which you prefer.

ii) Experiment with specific formatting requirements on a short piece of unimportant writing. Find out what your pc and Word can do. If you need help, your local computer shop or a friend who's computer-savvy can help. Don't risk ruining your work, and in any case, keep back-up copies of an unblemished manuscript, just in case.

Example

a) In the original version of *A Night With No Stars*, the poem below which heads Chapter 1, is presented in Mistral font 14, to resemble the writer's handwriting.

I.

Sacred land. Sidh of my soul with its springs
Of eternal youth. Whose waters return the stars'
Gaze, whose mirror traps the Glory of the Day
And turns His eye to gold...
R F J 1986

At six o'clock on a mid-June evening in London's Covent Garden, and so hot that even the pavements seemed to be sweating, Lucy Mitchell, twenty-nine year old assistant editor with the literary publishers Hellebore, passed through the hotel's automatic door and into its Art Deco-tiled foyer.

Chapter 50

What Could Spoil The Party?

Copyright issues. It's a litigious world out there, so be warned. Any copyrighted material originally published less than 70 years before you plan to use it, is a no-no unless you or your publisher are prepared to wait weeks for permission to be granted and pay. In *A Night with No Stars*, I naïvely used a verse from a Cole Porter song as a chapter heading. Fortunately, my publishers spotted it, and had to hand over $35 to Warner Bros. Not a lot, as WB generously understood I'd made a genuine error.

Look at publishers' disclaimers at the beginning of any recently published chiller thrillers. Also your own contract where you may have to pay legal fees against possible charges of blasphemy and slander.

Don't go there.

Portraying recognisable characters alive or dead in a damaging or controversial light in your fiction, can cause raised eyebrows or worse. In C.J. Sansom's latest historical thriller, *Dominion*, the late Lord Beaverbrook becomes Prime Minister and Enoch Powell is given the Secretary of State for India post in a German-occupied UK. A role his widow has apparently objected to, adding to the controversy. This can be a double-edged sword, yet I salute this writer for his bravery, and hope others are inspired by his imagination.

In *The Casual Vacancy*, JK Rowling had supposedly used village characters who were rather too close to home. One in particular, refers disparagingly to an Indian woman, and Rowling's lawyer claimed it was the *character*, not the author speaking. An interesting point! However, if you're unsure, take advice.

Never enter the world of 'sock puppetry' by anonymously or

with pseudonyms, posting deleterious reviews of other writers' work on Amazon and other online outlets. One well-known author did this for several years and was outed by furious fellow writing sleuths. Not a good career move. Neither is tax avoidance. Keep receipts for everything, from paperclips to train/airline tickets. Petrol receipts too, particularly if you've driven to Land's End to check out the waves. These will be tax deductable.

Exercises

i) Before sending off your submission, check through thoroughly for any of the above, and other potential stumbling blocks such as careless typos; incorrect dates for known events; poor research, and copyright hazards. Yes, a thorough agent or editor/copy-editor will be your safety net, but it's more professional if you sort out the problems first.

ii) On your reading travels, have you discovered any material that you yourself would never use? That made you wonder how the work had ever been published? This will help sharpen your own awareness.

Chapter 51

Agents' And Publishers' Contracts

Shouldn't I just put them in a drawer?

No! Scrutinise every word, however small the print, and don't be afraid to politely ask any questions about royalties, rights and author liabilities etc. If you're still unhappy, join the Society of Authors, who are extremely knowledgeable and helpful. I suggest you join them anyway.

The main publishing houses are still offering sizeable advances against royalties to debut writers, however, the norm is more modest and shrinking. Some, especially the smaller independent publishers offer none at all, but are getting your book out there at their expense. They are often more prepared to take risks with exciting new authors and be more communicative and supportive.

Only in rare cases should a writer hand over copyright for the full term, which is 70 years after your decease, but there are circumstances where granting copyright, for say, a limited period, may be useful to both parties. If you do, you should be paid. Several European publishers seem to take their authors' copyright as the norm, but again, make sure you are fully in the picture, and don't be pressured. There may be opportunities for your work to appear in large print format and on audio. Do ask about these, because large print versions are much borrowed by library users. As for myself, listening to the Soundings audio version of *Cloven* was a great experience. However, I hadn't bargained on Ivan Browning, one of its two main characters, having such a strong Irish accent! The producers had clearly picked up on the fact his parents still lived in Ireland.

All part of the publishing experience.

You may be lucky enough to land a two-book or even a three

or more book deal. In these uncertain times, this is some stability, however, remember that further down the line when seeking a new contract, if your last book didn't sell a substantial number of copies, you may, despite your very latest book being your best, be stranded.

When your book goes out of print, ask for rights to revert to you, preferably with a PDF version, which you may have to buy. If you part with these reverted rights to another publisher, there should be a proper contract and again, as for the copyright, you should be paid an agreed sum.

For detailed advice on contracts in more traditional publishing, you'll find everything you need to know in Michael Legat's thorough book, *An Author's Guide To Publishing*. Although not recent, it's still invaluable. More on-trend is *The Writers' & Artists' Yearbook* and the *Writers' Handbook* which annually include helpful articles on self-publishing, print on demand, short-run printing, e-publishing etc. Far more than I can mention here.

Meanwhile, if working with an agent and editor, be flexible to start with, then further down the line, you may have more control.

Chapter 52

So, You're Out There. Congratulations!

The roller-coaster starts now. How to stay on it, keep the faith and your sanity.

Try to see your writing and research as your most important activities. Like your chiller thriller itself, keeping the momentum going means limiting your online activity to one or two evenings a week, otherwise, it can swamp your inner life which you need for the gestation and realisation of new work. Be firm but polite with those who seek your constant attention. Author James Lasdun has a chilling story to tell on this one.

Today, image is everything, and a striking author photograph can help sell you and your book. Apparently, a well-known novelist of a certain age, lies on the floor for her author photos! You can digitally supply your own which should reflect the genre in which you write. For chiller thrillers, I'd suggest the chiaroscuro effect of dark and light contrasts, together with a relevant background. If you're published by a mainstream publisher, you may be fortunate enough to have a well-known, professional photographer take you to a suitable location. However, the page-turning thriller, *Eye Contact* (Hodder & Stoughton) has a great photo of its author, Fergus McNeill, taken by his teenage son.

Just before *Wringland* was published by Pan Macmillan, celebrity photographer, Jerry Bauer used St. Augustine's Gothic-style church in south Kensington as a backdrop for my author photo. Such a thrill.

Exercises

i)   Study several author photographs in their thrillers and on their websites.

ii) Do these add anything to your perceptions of the author? Do they enhance the book?

If you're published by a mainstream publisher, their publicist will hopefully do some leg work to organise a launch, garner reviews and the rest. Sadly, but realistically, it's usually the big hitters who get the bulk of marketing funds and the attention of newspaper reviewers. However, there's still plenty you, and your publisher - even if a small, independent one - can do.

My current publishers, Sparkling Books have been very supportive, while other authors with bigger publishers, are sometimes heard complaining. Whether you have an agent or not, *The Writers' Handbook*, *The Writers' & Artists' Yearbook* and *An Author's Guide to Publishing* by Michael Legat, should answer all your questions.

Chapter 53

Blogging And Bragging, Moi?

Absolutely. It's crucial, and if you have mobility or health problems, being in front of your computer is all you need to do. Even a launch party or two can be organised and held online.

Make full use of the latest social media to enhance your profile and if you're self-published, this could later attract the interest of an agent/publisher.

Being a pro-active author is every agent and publisher's dream. For yourself, if self-published whether in book form or on Kindle etc. it's even more necessary.

Do I Need A Website?

Yes. Ideally one that enables you to blog and in return, receive feedback via a Guest blog.

You can either pay a website designer to set this up for you, or do it yourself. Moonfruit provide a good service and it's free! Also Weebly. If finances are a problem, there may be a student in a graphic design department of a nearby Art College or University who could add its design to his/her CV as well as for you. I use the excellent website design company, Wave Seven, based in Northampton because I don't have the time to deal with continual additions and deletions. I hope the eerie ravens on my Home page and also the black and white photographs taken in France, reflect my dark subject matter.

Do have a CONTACT ME facility, an interesting LINKS list and a BLOGSPOT.

Exercises

i) Take a look at 6 other thriller writers' websites.

ii) What worked? What didn't? Why?

iii) Were they up to date? Were they clear and easy to navigate?

iv) Did any have a link to their own blog?

v) If not, find 3 blogs and read as much as you have time for. Are they self-absorbed or do they draw upon current affairs? The world of literature? Films etc? Do they present the writer in a memorable way? Do they actually address ideas? Include visuals?

John Connolly's blog is worth a look. It's welcoming and inclusive.

vi) Having done this, jot down what *you* would do. Which pitfalls to avoid.

vii) Explore free providers such as Moonfruit and Weebly for your own website.

viii) Get at least 3 quotes from reputable designers and/or reliable students.

Your website visuals and fonts should reflect your book and yourself. For a gritty, dangerous spy thriller, you're hardly going to use pink to promote it! Keep the website uncluttered and easy to use. This should include a CONTACT ME link and also links to any useful contacts you may have. E.g., The Crime Writers' Association; the International Association of Crime Writers; other authors similar to you. (Check first that they're happy for you to do this.) Other organizations whose activities could be influential in your writing e.g., the RSPCA or Dundee University with its pioneering new Department of Forensic Medicine. You decide...

Exercises

i) Examine the LINKS lists on your 6 chosen thriller writers' websites. You may find some useful for yourself and your own research.

ii) Make a list of all your interesting and useful contacts.

Add them and others' website/Facebook/Twitter links to your Links page.

Other Networking Possibilities

i) Business cards, bookmarks and postcards are all invaluable for spreading the word about your book and you. Your publisher may subsidise these with their logo writ large, if not, use your cover design for the visuals and typography for your postcard and bookmark, while your business card should reflect the mood of your work.

ii) The Next Big Thing MeMe is great to promote your upcoming book. Ask a published writer already using it to 'tag' you. I discovered that thriller writers Margaret Murphy and Adrian Magson had announced this on their Facebook pages and had tagged me and other writers to join in. I, in turn, will do the same.

iii) Start a daily/weekly blog on a writers' life, without giving too much away about your next book! Recently, a mother living on a farm and left on her own all week, began regularly blogging about her perceived abandonment. Eventually, a leading publisher snapped up her story. It does happen! The important thing is to be realistic and be reliable. Don't commit to a daily blog if you're going to have lengthy gaps. Weekly is better, and preferably just before the weekend. I've learnt a lot from blogs, especially where links to an interesting topic are given, plus genuine recommendations for books.

iv) Follow @mollygreene on Twitter. She's written a how-to guide on blogging, BLOG IT!

Twitter

Sparkling Books, publisher of my two most recent chiller

thrillers. helped me get started with Twitter. Despite its naysayers, to writers, publishers and reviewers, it's another wonder of the world. Not surprising that totalitarian governments live in fear of it. You are no longer at your desk chair, but 'meeting' other writers and everyone else doing every conceivable kind of work, or simply just being. If however, a follower is being tricky, block them. A 'troll' or two on your tail is no joke, and no one needs to suffer!

Exercises

i) Check out 4 other writers' names/imagery/tweets. Are you impressed? Can you do better?

ii) Register on Twitter. Upload an intriguing photo of yourself, ideally in a setting that reflects you/and or your book. And/or upload your book cover. Create a unique eye-catching 'page' for it all. Even your Twitter 'name' can reflect the book.

iii) Find and follow at least 6 authors in your genre, and 6 reviewers who read thrillers. If they reply, invite them to read your book and post a review. If your book is on Net Galley, then do give the link. www.netgalley.com. Likewise the link for your book on Amazon.

iv) Follow at least 6 others who can be useful.

v) Send out 6 tweets. Two of which are about your book.

vi) Always thank whoever follows you. This can lead to interesting exchanges and possible reviews. Especially online. Thanks to Twitter, I've had my books reviewed many times and been asked to do gigs. However, relentless self-promotion can be a turn-off. Be generous to others and avoid reckless controversy.

Intersperse your book news with other news/comment/information. As on Facebook, you'll find enough kindred spirits with whom to enjoy these interactions.

Facebook

Facebook gives more scope for imparting information, messages and images, not simply because there's no restrictive letter count as in Twitter, but because your Friends will generally be people you can trust. If someone you don't know requests to be your Friend, check them out first and ignore if you're not sure. As for Twitter, you can block them.

On a more positive note, you could, as an author, develop an Author Page, where you can keep everyone informed and send out invitations to your gigs. Waterstone's and other bookshops/author venues do this repeatedly. Check out Adrian Magson's Author Page as a good example.

As on Twitter, you'll find that your generosity and an interest in others will not only give you pleasure, but pay dividends.

Exercises

i)   Search for 6 writers and/or agents or editors you admire, and request to be their Friend.

ii) Upload photos of yourself and your book cover.

iii) Create an Author page.

iv) Mention another literary event that's not to do with you.

v)   Update at least monthly to keep things fresh.

LinkedIn

This seems to be growing in popularity, and again, can provide you with a helpful platform for your work and interests. Again, generosity to others can reap rewards. You can endorse contacts you've already met, for various professional skills.

Goodreads/Library Thing

Keep your profile updated, and your reviews and gradings coming in.

A great site on which to share work and ideas is www.thrill-skillsandchills.blogspot.co.uk.

Pinterest is an excellent online pinboard for reviews and recommendations.

Exercises

i) Research crime and thriller reviewers in specialist magazines and e-zines. E.g., *Mystery People, Eurocrime, Crime Squad, Crime Time, Reviewing the Evidence, Shots Mag* etc.

ii) Send their editors (get their names right!) a Press Release of your book and/or a short piece on yourself + photograph. Even if you don't get a response from them all, you can follow on Twitter. Re-tweet their news and generally keep your name bobbing about!
    The Big Thrill webzine for thriller readers regularly publishes paperback anthologies of short stories from invited writers. However, they do select several others for inclusion from general submissions.

iii) Join the Crime Writers' Association and enter their Debut Dagger Award. (Closing date is usually the end of February each year.) You can now join as a Provisional Member if you have a genuine contract.

iv) Submit your published book's cover and details for their Members' latest publications section. Also add your Facebook and Twitter links. All the information needed for this is on their site. www.thecwa.co.uk The CWA will also display the details of any forthcoming events.

v) Submit short stories for inclusion in the occasional CWA anthologies which are sold in most major retail outlets. It's from these anthologies that the CWA Short Story Dagger is often won.

vi) Link on to the CWA's Crime Readers' Association where you can read about fellow writers and also send in reviews. There's also an opportunity to reveal where you write etc.

vii) Contribute to the CWA's excellent *Red Herrings* monthly magazine by giving out your New Member details and penning an interesting article about how you got started, or any aspect of your writing life. If you are an expert in a particular field, that's always useful. Its editor welcomes new material.

viii) Join the International Thriller Writers' Inc. which is USA based. (First, check out their very discerning criteria for author's publishers.)

ix) If appropriate, join the Historical Novel Association. (USA) or,

x) Historical Writers' Association.

xi) Subscribe to a writing magazine. You can then submit an article about your success, offering advice to other aspiring writers.

xii) Subscribe to *Mystery People* (e-zine) and ask its wonderful editor, Lizzie Hayes if she'll promote your book. You can also write reviews of crime/thrillers for publication. This will also raise your profile, help your own writing, and keep this great magazine as successful as it is.

xiii) Attend CrimeFest in Bristol. It's usually held mid-May each year, and this international event is always exciting, with the ever-supportive Richard Reynolds of Blackwells eager to display and sell its participants' books. Best to reserve a place early if you want a panel slot, or an In The Spotlight opportunity. Myles Alfrey, Donna Moore and Adrian Muller are organisers *par excellence*. www.crimefest.com

xiv) The Theakston's Old Peculier Festival of Crime Writing held each July in Harrogate, is another opportunity for networking.

These events usually offer important awards for crime novels and thrillers, so it's worth encouraging your publisher to enter you for the relevant ones. The annual Wales Book of the Year awards are open to authors connected to the Principality. Self-published books are also accepted. Check out Literature Wales for details.

xv) The St. Hilda's Crime & Mystery Weekend, in Oxford each August. Mystery People has all the details.

xvi) Literature Wales is a supportive, pro-active organisation for Welsh writers. Check out your own region for similar opportunities.

Chapter 54

What Else Can I Do?

Public Libraries

Too long taken for granted and many are now in peril. If you get the chance to sign any anti-closure petitions, please do it! Writers often depend on their Public Lending Right money to survive. Even now, the Government is planning to cut the lending fee to authors.

Traditionally, libraries have only taken hardback editions because of their durability, but this is changing. My recent trade paperbacks are happily reinforced by plastic covers. Your publisher will arrange library distribution through Gardner's and Bertram's, but make sure you register your title/s - if in print format - for PLR in the UK and Ireland before the end of June each year. The maximum you can earn is £5,000.

When I was first published in 2001, I teamed up with two other new crime/thriller writers and Hazard Warning was the result. We not only received a very welcome Arts Council grant to tour the UK, but we created a lot of new material for public performance and found libraries in particular, very happy to showcase us.

Exercises

i)   Contact all public libraries in your area. Go and meet the librarian in charge of events. Offer to give a talk/workshop using a crowd-pulling title. There may be other published authors - even writing in different genres – who could join you. Not so daunting as going solo! Don't expect a large fee because sadly, many libraries are struggling. If planning to work with young people, you'll need a CRB check, which can take some time.

ii) If you're published in print format, join the Authors Licensing & Copyright Society (ALCS). They do a brilliant job of collecting fees paid from the reproduction of your work. Check their website and register online. Or by post. Again, their annual payment is always welcome.

Readers' Groups

If your book is in print format, it's well worth asking your nearest library if there are any in your area. They're guaranteed to include an interesting mix of well-read members who enjoy nothing more than lively discussion on the latest book they've been assigned to read. And the next one could be yours! If you also have connections further afield, then try there too. Whilst living in Northampton, I was assigned two conjoined readers' groups up in Bottesford. As their members know, my journeys to and from the pub where we met, were always full of incident and peculiar weather. As for the venue itself, that was worthy of any chiller thriller, what with a headless airman haunting the disused aerodrome, and infamous sister witches buried in a local graveyard.

As I've said earlier, nothing is wasted…

Exercises

i) Ask the organiser of a local readers' group if they'd be happy to read your new book. Nothing ventured, and the worst you'll get is silence!

ii) Make an effort to get to meet your local newspaper editor/s with your news of your new publication. Face to face is aways ideal.

iii) Call into any bookshops in your area. Speak to the manager and ideally, the buyer. Not all booksellers possess Richard Reynolds' (Blackwell's, Cambridge) zeal and dedication to authors, but selling yourself and your new book can't simply be left to your publisher. If your book is set outside your area, contact any media outlets related to it. I've found this to be a good move. Real, recognisable settings are great 'hooks.'

iv) Many regions in the UK have their own local radio stations. Again, like libraries, I have found programmers to be extremely helpful and willing to give me air time. Interviews can either be done from home via telephone, or in the studio. Here on BBC Radio Wales, chiller writer Phil Rickman has his own show, 'Phil the Shelf' which, because of his probing questions, has become very popular.

v) Upload an eye-catching video on to YouTube of you reading from your book, or if possible, in one of its settings.

vi) If there are any CWA 'Chapter' meetings within travelling distance, then try and go. They are always convivial occasions, and a fount of useful information and gossip!

Use Google or Dogpile - an excellent search engine - to look for other Writing Festivals/Conferences. e.g.; Winchester Writers' Conference; York Festival of Writing; Bouchercon (USA) Left Coast Crime (USA)

Fresh blood (excuse the expression,) is always welcomed!

vii) News just in of the World Science-Fiction Convention taking place this year in London. Details from - http://www.loncon3.org

Entering Competitions

As already mentioned in chapter 9, there's nothing like a win or a place to frank your credentials. If a door marked 'chance' is ajar, push it open. Scour online listings for suitable competitions that don't discriminate against genre fiction. Most writing magazines run regular competitions, and there are many more to try. Read the rules carefully. Check who's judging and avoid sending out last minute.

At the time of writing, DC Thompson publishers are looking for crime/thrillers of 50,000 words. They promise lots of marketing. Enquire with a synopsis and first 3 chapters to; easyread @dcthompson.co.uk.

Macmillan publishers are currently running a novel competition for the YA market, and Chapter One Promotions' Blood Ink' crime writing competition ends in November.

Chapter 55

Useful Reference Books And Magazines

Inside the Mind of a Killer – On the trail of Francis Heaulme by Jean-Francois Abgrall

Work Like a Spy by J.C. Carleson.

The Complete Encyclopedia of Terrorist Organizations by Paul Ashley

Freud, Insight and Change by Ilham Dilman

Bizarre Behaviours by Herschel Prins

The Lust to Kill by Deborah Cameron & Elizabeth Frazer

The Psychology of Cyberspace by John Suler

The Nurture Assumption by Judith Rich Harris

Cold Case Research by Silvia Pettem

Practical Crime Scene Processing and Investigation by Ross M. Gardner

http://forensics4fiction by Tom Adair

The Dictionary of Magic and Mystery by Melusine Draco (Kindle)

A Dictionary of Superstitions by D. and M.A Radford

Ghosts and How to see Them by Peter Underwood

Brewer's Dictionary of Phrase and Fable

The Oxford Dictionary of Quotations

The Physics of Immortality by Frank J. Tipler

Adventures in Time by Andrew Mackenzie

Triumph of the Embryo by Louis Wolpert

In the Blood. God, Genes and Destiny by Steve Jones

The Greatest Secret by David Icke

Specialist journals. E.g., farming/ antiques/ Tarot cards, etc

The Scientific American

Postscript books (Not a book club. Their books are fascinating and esoteric. All at bargain prices.)

Solutions for Novelists by Sol Stein

Solutions for Writers by Sol Stein (Non-fiction too.)

On Writing by Stephen King

Write On! by Adrian Magson. (pb and E-book)

Write to be Published by Nicola Morgan. (E-book.)

Tweet Right – The Sensible Person's Guide to Twitter by Nicola Morgan. (E-book.)

Dear Agent – Write the Letter that Sells Your Book by Nicola Morgan

An Author's Guide to Publishing by Michael Legat

The Writers' Handbook.

The Writers' & Artists' Yearbook

The New Writer

Writers' Forum

Writers News

Writing Magazine

Mslexia

Fiction Writers' Mentor (online)

Acknowledgments

Sally Spedding wishes to gratefully acknowledge the co-operation of her publishers Sparkling Books in permitting various excerpts from her following titles, *Wringland, Cloven, A Night With No Stars, Come and Be Killed, Cold Remains* and *Malediction*, to be included in this book.

www.sparklingbooks.com

Also, the literary agent John Jarrold for his quotation in my Introduction.

To Graham Hurley for his quotation in the Introduction.

To Adrian Magson for his quotation in Section 10, taken from a Big Thrill interview with Tom Adair.

Other grateful acknowledgments are due to the following authors who have kindly allowed me to use relevant examples of their books.

Author Name	Title	Page no.
Sarah Rayne Simon&Schuster	*Spider Light*	21/2 e-bk
Suzanne Ruthven Ignotus Press	*Whittlewood*	71/2 e-bk
Sarah Rayne Simon& Schuster	*Spider Light*	93/4 e-bk
Suzanne Ruthven Ignotus Press	*Whittlewood*	67/8e-bk
David Evans	*Torment*	111/2
Lorna Fergusson Fictionfire Press	*The Chase*	133/4 e-bk
Julie-Ann Corrigan	*Isabella's War*	140/1/2
David Evans	*Torment*	142/3/4
Suzanne Ruthven Ignotus Press	*Whittlewood*	147/8/9/150 e-bk

David Evans	*Trophies*	152/153
FeedaRead		
Julie-Ann Corrigan	*Isabella's War*	153/4/5
Julie-Ann Corrigan	*Falling Suns*	163
Sarah Rayne	*Spider Light*	174/5/6 e-bk
Simon& Schuster		
Julie-Ann Corrigan	*Falling Suns*	180/1
Lorna Fergusson	*The Chase*	218 e-bk
Fictionfire Press		

Other Titles by by Sally Spedding

Wringland
Cloven
A Night With No Stars
Prey Silence
Come and be Killed
Strangers Waiting
Cold Remains
Malediction

PRAISE FOR SALLY SPEDDING

'Her writing is so distinctly unique it will truly chill you to
the bone.'
Sally Meseg 'Dreamcatcher.'

'Spedding knows that before delivering the set-pieces, it's
essential to carefully build suspense theough both unsettling
incident and sense of locale – at both, she's unquestionably
got what it takes.'
Barry Forshaw 'Crime Time.'

'*Malediction* is an intense, intelligent, visceral thriller from
the get-go....Dark, dark fiction – definitely not for the
squeamish. If you thought Dan Brown was the last word in
clerical depravity, think again,'
Peter Guttridge Crime/thriller writer and reviewer

www.sallyspedding.com

**COMPASS
BOOKS**

Compass Books focuses on practical and informative 'how-to'
books for writers. Written by experienced authors who also have
extensive experience of tutoring at the most popular creative
writing workshops, the books offer an insight into the more
specialised niches of the publishing game.